Soy Sauce, Sugar, Mirin

Stop Paying for Teriyaki Sauce
and Other Kitchen Pro Tips

DRINK MORE WATER, MIKA!

[signature] ♡

by Harvard Wang

Designed, Written, Photographed, Published by
Harvard Wang

@harvardwang
soysaucesugarmirin.com

Special thanks to SAC for making this book possible.
Special thanks to Robyn Young for kinda proofreading.

During the COVID-19 lockdown in 2020, I shared a Japanese curry recipe on the 'Subtle Asian Cooking' Facebook group. It gathered two thousand likes overnight, encouraging me to self-publish the recipes into a physical book.

Within 15 days, I sold out 500 copies to America, Canada, Ireland, London, Paris, Finland, Singapore, Malaysia, Taiwan, even Geelong.

This book is my second print run.

So here goes →

Contents

I Hate Coffee Table Cookbook.

They are made for, well, the coffee table - mostly written by ghostwriters who did not make the dishes, edited by editors who did not taste the dishes, photographed by photographers who care only about the lighting - not the *taste* of the food.

I know this, because I'm a food photographer.

I'm not saying don't buy beautiful cookbooks, just that they are often impractical, sometimes too much dough and not enough filling, like a soggy spring roll, a cold bao, an oversized borek.

<u>So, this is not a coffee table book.</u>

I grew up in Malaysia, live in Australia and my wife is Japanese. The recipes in this book may be best described as 'all over the place, with a hint of coffee snobbery, leaning towards Asian fermented seafood'.

These are 40 real, practical dishes I've been making for my real, practical family and friends for the last 10 years. Included are the little short cuts and pro tips I gathered along the way through painful trial and error.

These recipes work to my taste, not necessarily yours.

So <u>taste, adapt, improvise</u>, make them your own.

<u>This is a simple book about cooking.</u>

There are no stories about my childhood, no 'moments' and 'inspiration' paired with beautiful yet pointless photographs of lemons in a fruit bowl. This book will not teach you how to dice onions, peel potatoes, or boil pasta. There's a place for that - the internet.

The two most important pieces of equipment you need to use this book are <u>your tongue</u>, to taste, and <u>your brain</u>, to judge and adjust.

You should be able to make all the dishes with basic kitchen utensils. Although, it'd be ideal for you to own a pressure cooker, cast iron pot, a solid cooking pan, a trustworthy knife, digital timer, scale and thermometer. If you have an air-fryer or a thermomix, get your servants to read this.

Just remember, this is not a coffee table book.

It's made for the kitchen bench.

I hope you treat it with disrespect.

Traditional Dashi.

Dashi literally translates to 'excreted juice'.
Sexy, I know.

It is made from 3 ingredients - water, dried kelp (kombu),
and shaved bonito flakes (katsuobushi). All available from
Japanese & Asian grocery stores.

Think of the 'excreted juice' as umami water. It is the
lifestream of all Japanese cooking.

Bring a pot of 500ml water to boil, then turn the heat off.
Drop a 10g piece of kelp (2% of water weight) into the
water, seep for 10 minutes, remove the kelp. Bring the
water back to boil, heat off*.
Add 10g (2% of water weight) worth of bonito flakes**.
Steep for 10 minutes. Strain.

This is your umami water.

Outside of Japan, we're all paying premium for generic
brands of konbu and bonito flakes, and there's a big chance
your restaurant dashi came in a commercial 10L tin. Even
the Japanese in their Japanese home rarely make dashi
from scratch anymore. The fact you're trying means you're
well ahead of the curve.
Be proud.

Proper dashi is better than dashi soup pack is better than powder dashi is better than stock cube is better than water.

Here's a hack: soup packs in Asian groceries. There's the soluble powdered packs (Drake says no) and the tea packs (Drake says that's better). If you can score some *Kayanoya* brand dashi pack, do it. It's not cheap, but good things seldom are.

Boil 400ml water, throw the pack in and simmer for 2-3 minutes, and voila, instant umami water.

Use for miso soup, oden, nikujaga, stew, hot pot, tamagoyaki, noodles, stir fries, congee, ramen, curry, soba dips ...

* The Japanese think boiling water ruins everything - the kelp will go bitter and slimy, bonito flakes will smell, miso will DIE. So they always insist on 'seeping' the ingredients in 80°C. But if you accidentally forget, don't fret, man.

** Once I asked a Japanese ryokan chef how much bonito flakes is too much. He replied: double the amount you think you need, and then double it again.

Super Boring Miso Soup for 2.

Bring 400ml of dashi to boil, add cubed tofus*.

Switch off the heat once the tofu cubes start to 'dance'.
Add 1.5 tbsp of miso paste - red, white, mixed, all good.

Pro tip: <u>push a small whisk into the miso</u> and stir the miso
from the whisk into the pot straight away. That's one less
utensil to wash up.

Taste, adjust miso. Taste again.

The secret to a good bowl of miso soup is to simply taste
and adjust until it hits the note you're after.

If you have solid dashi and miso, you simply can't make
bad miso soup.

Once you're satisfied, add spring onions, wakame**.

It's so boring, you should be having this every morning.

* Use silken tofu for better mouthfeel; firm tofu for deeper flavour.

** There are endless possibilites with miso soup other than the
default tofu and spring onions. Try carrots, mushrooms, egg drop,
cabbage, shredded tofu puffs, corn, fish cakes, spinach, potatoes,
shredded chicken, shrimp, clams ...

* I honestly don't think the type of miso (red or white, whatever) matters as long as it's good quality. If you don't have miso - doubanjiang, tianmianjiang, gochujiang, char siu sauce, anything soy fermented should work. Just taste and adjust. I bet you could even substitute eggplant with zucchini, tomatoes, mushrooms... Think of it like cheese on toast, but miso gravy on vegetables.

Oven, Miso, Eggplant.

Ladies, if your date orders this dish for you at a restuarant, he's totally into you. Trust me, the only reason one would learn to pronounce 'nasu dengaku' is to woo the other half, like a flamingo dancing during mating season.

Slice an eggplant in half, score the flesh into little squares and place them skin side down on a tray. Drizzle with oil and place in 180°C oven for 15 minutes or so.

While you wait, make the sauce - bring 4 parts (tbsp) miso*, 2 parts water, 1 part sugar, 1 part mirin, 1 part sake to simmer for 5 minutes or until thickened. Taste the sauce. It should be on the saltier side because the eggplant will absorb most of it. If you want you can add some soy sauce or fish sauce. Like sweet stuff? Add sugar. Too thick? Add more water.

Check the eggplant with a knife - it should glide through. Brush your miso paste like frosting on cake, set the oven to broil (top grill) for 2-3 minutes. I'm a big fan of crispy burnt bits but of course, you can adjust to your liking. The miso paste should be bubbling. Bubble = good.

Pro tip - add some shredded cheese.

Sprinkle some sesame seeds if you bother. We usually eat with a spoon like eating mango. Sometimes, thick eggplants gets watery inside and I don't see anything wrong with it. Instant miso soup with eggplant juice.

If you have leftover sauce, save it for soup, curry, toast, stir fry. Or just make another eggplant.

The Perfect Onsen Egg.

<u>The Japanese Way:</u>

Go to a hot spring in Japan, put eggs in a net, drop into the onsen, peel and eat after you're done with your bath.

You say: screw that you poor-man-David-Chang-Adam-Liaw-wannabe, we're under a travel ban.

<u>Okay, this is from *Anova*:</u>

Sous vide eggs at 63°C for 60 minutes.

You say: screw that you geek, who has a sous-vide machine?

<u>Okay, this is from Ivan Orkin:</u>

Prepare 4 large eggs at room temperature. Bring a pot of water (enough to cover your eggs by 2cm) to boil, switch off the heat, add 20% cold water, lower eggs, wait for 12-13 minutes, then plunge into an ice bath.

You say: screw that you gaijin-lover, I keep my eggs in the fridge; not room temperature, eww.

Okay, this is from *Just One Cookbook*:

Bring 1L of water to boil, switch off the heat, add 200ml cold water, lower cold eggs for 17 minutes, remove, set aside for 15 minutes.

You say: screw that, that's 30 minutes in total, I might as well sous vide.

Okay, this is from *Serious Eats*:

Get a thermometer, bring water in pot to 75°C. Lower eggs and make sure water stays at 75°C for 13 minutes. Remove eggs, plunge into an ice bath.

You say: screw that, I'm the CMO of a company! I don't have time to stand around and stare at a thermometer for 13 minutes.

Okay, this is from *Subtle Asian Cooking* Comment #49

Crack and submerge an egg in water, put in the microwave on medium and zap with 30-second intervals until the way you like it.

You say: screw that, microwave gives you cancer.

Okay, how about comment #122 and #159:

 ← Buy a Malaysian soft-boiled egg maker.

You say: screw that, plastic gives you cancer! Also, does my home look like a *Kopitiam* to you?

<u>Okay, this is from me:</u>

Prepare half a dozen of eggs. Label them 1 to 6.

Bring 1L water to boil, switch off the heat, and add 200ml cold water.

Drop all eggs and set a timer. At the 12 minute mark, take egg 1 out into an ice bath. At the 12:30 minute mark remove egg 2, at 13 minute mark remove egg 3, repeat.

Once all the eggs are done, crack the eggs in separate bowls. Pick your favourite, and from now on, you buy the same eggs, from the same shop, cook them with the same pot, with the same amount of water, for the same amount of time.

And that, is how you get perfect Onsen Tamago.

You say: screw that ......

Sexy Ramen Eggs.

Can you count to <u>six</u>?

Prepare <u>six</u> eggs.

Bring a pot of water (enough to cover the eggs) to boil.

<u>Poke a tiny hole on top of the fat end of the eggs.</u>

How? Use a thumbtack, or be like a Japanese housewife and buy an egg piercer from Daiso*. The hole acts like a little escape hatch so that the pressure can equalize in the egg and prevent the eggshell from cracking. This is super important. Ramen restaurants do this in Japan.

So remember: <u>six</u> eggs, <u>six</u> holes.

Slowly lower the eggs into the water once boiling -
I like seeing the air bubbles coming out of the hole.
I tell my daughter the eggs are farting and we giggle.

Immediately set the timer to <u>six</u> minutes. (Seven if you want the yolks firmer. I wouldn't go above eight.)

Prepare an ice bath.

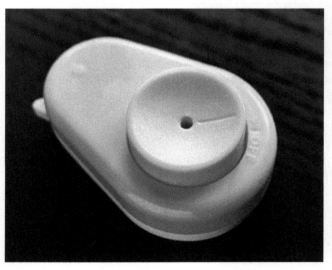

* A Daiso egg-piercer

Keep an eye on the water - we want the water to boil constantly but not so much that the eggs knock into the pot / each other.

While you wait, whisk <u>six</u> tbsp of soy sauce, <u>six</u> tbsp of mirin, pour into a container or a ziplock bag.

When the time is up, plunge eggs into the ice bath for another <u>six</u> minutes. This is also important. No ice bath = no runny yolks. It will also make them easier to peel so you get Snow White eggs instead of Quasimodo eggs.

Peel the eggs. Knock the egg around the bench <u>six</u> times, and peel under running water. The ice bath should've made it easier to peel, but still, be gentle.

The eggs are ready to be consumed, but we're civilised people with will power, so we place the eggs into the container / ziplock bag together with the soy sauce mixture, top up with water until fully submerged.

Let them marinate for at least <u>six</u> hours or overnight in the refrigerator.

Eat it with or without ramen.
Eat it on your toast.
Eat it with your salad, your pizza, your leftover rice.
With or without your clothes on.

* Make stir-fry udon (yakiudon). Add into salad as a carb buffer. I've seen people eat udon mixed with a raw egg and chilli oil in Japan. I've seen people make carbonara with udon on Japanese TV. I personally have defrosted half a block of frozen udon and served it cold to my daughter. Shh.

Frozen Udon is Good Udon.

You can try to make udon from scratch, but you will hate yourself, and then you'll hate udon. Udon is innocent.

As of 2020 in Melbourne, a frozen 5-pack Maruchan udon costs $7. Compared to what you're paying for in a restaurant for essentially the same thing, it's a bargain. Feel free to explore other brands,

Prep 2 pots. One filled with water and the other with 400ml of dashi. Once the dashi comes to boil, add your toppings - chicken, tofu, mushroom, carrot, cabbage, lotus root. Feeling fancy? Prawns, scallops, calamari, fish slices...

Once the ingredients are cooked through, add three BIG handful of katsuobushi, heat off. Since udon noodles are slightly thicker, the stock should be stronger in flavour. Add a tbsp of soy sauce, a tsp of sugar. A tsp of tsuyuu or fish sauce won't hurt too. Taste. Adjust. Strain.

In the other boiling pot of water, drop a block of frozen udon, wiggle with your chopsticks. If you like your udon chewy and al dente, strain immediately once the noodles come undone. If you're a softie, wait another minute or two. Remember, the noodles are already cooked, we're just reheating it*. Pro tip: you can also microwave the frozen udon on medium for 3-4 minutes, then rinse with cold water. Set aside.

Add udon into the dashi pot. Top with an onsen egg / ramen egg / fried egg. Scatter with spring onions. Sprinkle with togarashi, cut chilli.

Slurp slurp.

Onion skins maketh golden stock.

* The meat should fall off the wings after making the stock.
Save them. Mix with 2 tbsp kewpie mayo, diced dill pickles.
They make great filling for cheese toasties.
** The secret to 'golden' chicken stock is not within the chicken;
but the onion skin and carrot.

Any Stock Is Better Than Water.

Dashi isn't cheap to make, and not everyone loves it.
But any stock is better than water. Here are some other
alternatives. Remember to freeze the leftover stock.
Bonus if you use an ice cube tray.

Easy chicken stock

Bring 500g of chicken wings to boil with 0.75L water,
skim the scum for the first 10-15 minutes. Pressure
cook for 45 minutes, quick release. If you don't have a
pressure cooker, simmer for 2 - 6 hours. Remember to
top up the water as you go. Strain*.

Golden chicken stock

After making easy chicken stock, toss in half a carrot, half
an onion with the skin on**, one stick of celery, two cloves
garlic and a knob of ginger. Seep for 45 minutes. Strain.
If you still want to elevate it, debone a whole chicken and
use the carcass additonal to the chicken wings. You want
to make it jelly like? Add chicken feet. I've basically given
you a chicken ramen stock recipe here.

Vegetable stock

Bring 1L water to boil, heat off. Seep half an onion with
the skin, half a carrot, one stick of celery, two cloves
garlic and a knob of ginger for 45 minutes. Strain.

Stock cubes

Powder, granules, soup packets, all good. The useful
thing about stock cube is you can find seafood stock and
vegetable stock ready to go. No judgement here.

Hipster
Croque-Madame au Poulet.

Everytime I make chicken stock, I know I'll be having cheese toastie the next day.

Because after straining the stock, I tear off all the meat that's left on the bones, mix together with plenty of kewpie mayo, 1 tsp of mustard, a great pinch of salt, finely-diced dill pickle and some leftover herbs like coriander or spring onions. Sometimes, I add curry powder or chilli flakes.

It's hipster because we're recycling, because reducing wastage, because eco-friendly. Get it?

So, melt a tbsp of butter on a medium heat frying pan, drop 2 pieces of sliced bread, soaking up some of the butter. Flip the bread. Place some melting cheese (I mix cheddar, Provolone, Edam) followed by the chicken mayo mixture on one slice of bread, cover with the other slice. Turn heat down to medium-low.

If you're 'jungle' like me, place a heavy pan / pot / kettle on top of the sandwich, wait for 1-2 minute.
If you're 'urban', use a sandwich press.

Flip, place weight, wait for another minute or two.

If you can't hear the crunch when you cut into the sandwich, you are doing it wrong. Better luck next time.

Fry an egg on top, or eat it as a croque-monsieur au poulet.

Scan here to buy real shokupan in Melbourne.

Tamago Sando is Egg, Bread.

Tell your daughter: " Today's lunch is egg and bread."
She stares at you before asking what time her mum and
future-stepfather are coming to pick her up.

Say: "Honey bunny, shall we make some tamago sando
for lunch? "

"Yatta! ", she says, " Papa daisuki! Can I also have some
ringo juice? "

Tamago (egg) sando (sandwich) is exactly that - egg and
bread. I know that. You know that. She doesn't have to.

Now there are some tricks to get the egg sandwich
to look and feel like the ones you see in Japanese
convenience stores.

<u>You need white fluffy bread.</u>

If you're in Melbourne, my friend Satoshi bakes shokupan
exclusively for sandwich specialty shops. Shokupan, so
hot right now - last I heard there's a white guy making
a sourdough version in South Melbourne. Sometimes,
Fujimart stock them too.

"Screw that, I don't live in Melbourne," you say.

Alright, buy a block of white bread from
Bakers Delight. I think they're called *Cobbs Bread* in the
US and Canada.

You're cringing. Don't cringe.

There's a one-hat restaurant in Melbourne famous for their lobster rolls. They are quite open that their buns are from - drum roll - Bread Top. (Equivalent to Bread Talk in Singapore.)

So don't be a snob, a fresh loaf from Bakers Delight or Bread Top is still better than a stale or burnt organic one. Go Wonderbread if you have to. Let's not teach our kids to be picky with food.

Now here comes the pro tip:

1. <u>Don't slice the bread too thick.</u>
I know that's the first instinct, but unless your filling is going to be thicker than the bread combined, you'll end up with a dry mouth. If that's how you like it, my bad. Carry on.

2. <u>Butter the bread generously.</u>
Especially if you're making katsu sando with lots of sauce. This creates a 'barrier' between the bread and fillings. Ever wondered why your sandwich gets all soggy and sad? Today you learned.

3. <u>Once you make your sando, WAIT.</u>
Sandwich the sandwich between two plates for 5 minutes while you make a pot of tea. Ever had a sandwich with cabbage and corn bits falling apart? You didn't wait, that's why. The weight makes sure the bread hugs the fillings nice and tight, like the one your daughter will give you after she tastes a proper tamago sando.

"What about the eggs?" You ask.

Come on, dad. Bring a couple of eggs in a pot of water to boil. Heat off, cover for 10 minutes. Shock in an ice bath, peel in a bowl, shell off, break and whisk with a fork. Add plenty of mayonnaise and softened butter. Cream if you have some in the fridge. Season with salt, taste. Season again. Grate some parmesan cheese.

If your daughter is fancy, finely chop some dill pickles or green herbs into the mix.

After you made hers, add some chilli/curry powder/ mustard into yours.

Some people prefer the bread crusts off. I teach my girl to appreciate the beauty of the Maillard reaction.

If you do cut them off, <u>don't throw the crusts away</u>. Bake them into croutons, pulse into breadcrumbs. Kids will eat anything crunchy.

Don't screw this up.

But most importantly, don't be a jerk.

What you feed her is not as important as how you treat her.

This insignificant egg sandwich will be a precious cornerstone memory for the both of you.

Shoyu
Satō
Mirin

Stop Paying for Teriyaki Sauce.

Soy sauce, sugar, mirin.

Repeat after me - soy sauce, sugar, mirin.

<u>1 part soy sauce, 1 part sugar, 1 part mirin.</u>

If you want to be fancy, add 1 part sake or any cooking wine of your choice.

Bring to a slow simmer for 10 minutes or until the desired consistency. It should be foaming towards the end. Be careful though, if you overcook it you'll end up with caramel. (Still nice with ice cream, though. Mmm teriyaki ice cream~)

That's pretty much it.
Say it again, soy sauce, sugar, mirin.
Make a litre and keep it in the fridge. It should last for 3-4 weeks. (But I keep it for 2-3 months. Shh.)

Toss it together with fried chicken, brush it over your sous vide ribeye. Drizzle it over your roasted kipfler, add mayonnaise and you have a dip for your crackers, celery sticks, fat chips. Hi sir, have you considered our lord and saviour steamed vegetables? Pan-fried salmon? Stir-fried noodles? Pizza sauce? In fact, apply it on anything your child won't eat. Like sunscreen.

The general rule of thumb of a recipe: the fewer the ingredients, the higher the quality. Not telling you to spend $25 on some organic soy sauce hand-pressed by Japanese mermaids, but don't use $2 Pearl River soy sauce and complain, mmkay?

But the takeaway here is <u>sugar</u>.

Both sugar and mirin give this sauce that thick, glossy viscosity. *Teri* (照り) means shiny, *yaki* (焼き) means grilling. Ever feel like your teriyaki sauce is lacking something compared to the restaurants? Just add sugar. In fact, most restaurants don't make their own teriyaki sauce anymore - they come in giant tin cans with stabilisers and preservatives and who knows what.

Sugar, man. Every time I add an insane amount of sugar, my wife would say 'mm this taste like home, your Japanese cooking has improved, fufufu'. Dude I just gave you diabetes, fufufu.

Different types of sugar - brown, honey, demerara, rapadura, muscovado will also affect the depth of your teriyaki sauce. But start with plain white before you learn to fly, yea?

Want to take it to the next level? Add grated garlic or ginger. Add tsuyuu. Replace sake with whiskey. Add mango chutney, jam. I remember *Shoya*, this old fancy Japanese restaurant along Market Lane, Chinatown had marmalade in their teriyaki chicken.

Deeper? How about sriracha? Sambal, gochujang, fish sauce, hoisin sauce, oyster sauce, five-spice powder. Add truffle if you want. You can't screw up a teriyaki sauce. If teriyaki sauce is a blood type it would be type O.

I'm not saying Japanese restaurants are ripping you off, but the next time you see the word 'teriyaki' on the menu going for twenty-odd bucks, remember:

<u>Soy sauce, sugar, mirin.</u>

How To Make Potasala.

Do you know how to walk into an Asian grocery store and look for Kewpie mayonnaise? Perform a transaction with the cashier? Online shopping?

Do you know how to pick potatoes? The yellow ones? Do you know how to gauge 1 potato per family member? Peel, then cut them into wedges, then boil in water and check doneness with a fork? Or, fill with water in a bowl and cover with cling film then microwave for 7-8 minutes. Do you know how to tip the hot water out without burning yourself? Do you know how to mash potato? With some cream, butter, milk and the Kewpie mayonnaise you bought?

Do you know how to incorporate some crunch into your silky mashed potato? How to finely dice half a carrot? Core some cucumber then slice them into tiny wedges? Or just peel them into ribbons? Do you know how to buy nice ham - champagne ham, grandmother ham, or even nicer, some San Daniele *prosciutto*? How about sausages from the supermarket? Bacon? Dice and pan fry them until crispy?

Do you know how make hard-boiled eggs?

How to microwave a stalk of corn covered with a wet kitchen paper on high for 5 minutes, then cutting it off the cob without burning your hand?

Do you know how to throw everything in a bowl and mix with a spoon?

The foundation of
Japanese Potato Salad
is potatoes (duh)
and Kewpie Mayo.
The rest is simply
free-styling.

Do you know how to taste the potato salad and season it with salt and pepper? How about a tsp of mustard? Grate some cheese? Chop up some herbs? Sprinkle some sichimi togarashi or chilli powder?

Add more Kewpie mayo, butter, cream?

Then, you know how to make a Japanese potato salad.

 Did you know: there is a Japanese Potato Salad Association? Their goal is to connect people with Potasala. Awww.

Korokke Express.

Unless you have a wife who ~~demands~~ kindly requests you to make them from scratch for her birthday, I think korokke should be renamed as 'deep fried mashed potato balls with yesterday's leftovers'.

Pro tip: <u>make mashed potatoes, then mix in leftovers.</u> The norm is to add sautéed diced onions and minced beef, but why bother if you already have leftover potasala from yesterday?

Sometimes I use leftover fish and chop up some parsley with the potatoes. Sometimes, pasta sauce and cheese to make pizza balls. Sometimes, I use mapo tofu leftover.

Also, the typical flour > egg > panko coating steps take up too much kitchen space and time for me, so pro tip: <u>whisk 1 egg, 50g water and 50g cake flour to form a 2-in-1 batter</u>.

Roll your mashed potatoes into balls, coat with the batter, then panko and deep-fry to golden. Since everything's already cooked, all we are looking for is colour. Alternatively, spray with oil then oven bake at 180°C for 20 minutes.

Don't waste your leftover batter and panko either - make ham katsu, spam katsu, smashed peas katsu, eggplant katsu. Why not finish up overnight rice - Asian Arancini? Why not Ice cream?

~~My child~~ I will eat ANYTHING deep fried.

Kale Chips.

These technically aren't chips, but they are crispy and calling them chips is easier to coax my daughter into eating them.

Preheat a <u>fan-forced oven</u> to 120°C. Once, I chose the non-fan mode by mistake and it just wouldn't crisp up.

Remove the stems by cutting a V shape around the ribs, soak, rinse and (very importantly) spin dry.

We are going to dehydrate the leaves so having water really defeats the purpose. I usually use half of the bunch and keep the other half for later in the week for stir fries / juice.

Lay the kale leaves on a tray with baking paper and drizzle with olive oil. <u>Pro tip: really scrunch and massage the oil over all the leaves</u>. Make them shiny shimmering splendid.

Place in the middle rack of the oven. 15 minutes later, turn and move the kale around with tongs and leave for another 10 minutes. If it's still soggy at some parts then give it another 5 minute or so. I usually turn off the oven as I finish off other dishes.

When they're crisp to your liking, serve in a bowl. You can salt it, but the taste is already quite intense. Grated cheese is good. Chilli powder, sichimi, garam masala also good. You wanna dip in mayo? Go crazy.

Massage the kale
like you mean it.

The quality of kale will greatly affect the taste and texture. Obviously avoid the ones that are turning yellow. Don't get tricked by the markets as they spray water and make vegetables look nicer than they really are.

Smell them. Sometimes you get this mouldy scent and that's a no-no. Fresh ones come out thinner, crispier, more vibrant in colour.

Trust your own nose and instinct.

Asian Greens.

Asians don't eat salads. We merely order them to fit in.

I'm not going to be the condescending uncle,
Asian-splaining how to stir-fry vegetables.

But here are my tips:

1. Before you go all 'wok hero' with the greens, <u>blanch them in salted water for 30 seconds</u>, then shock in ice bath. The goal is to pre-cook the greens and bring out the colours before you toss them over high heat. You can do this way ahead and chill in the fridge until you need to serve them.

2. A French chef taught me to use a scrubbing pad to scrub off the outer layers of asparagus, carrots, parsnips etc to make them smooth yet still keeping the outer layer intact. Very classy. Much fine dining.

3. If you're using gai lan or something stalk heavy, <u>cook the stalks</u> first, for an extra minute or so.

Garlic, soy sauce, dried chillis are perfect for me.

But dried shrimps, oyster sauce, belachan... all good.

The One Salad I Make.

Fine, sometimes we simply can't escape salads. What if you're assigned to bringing one to a potluck? Fear not. This salad is the only reason I buy quinoa because it's almost passable as rice. Easily replaceable with actual cooked rice, beans, barley, lentils, soba noodles, egg noodles, rice noodles.

Dressing: Whisk 2 part olive oil to 1 part lime juice with a splash of balsamic vinegar and a tsp each of mustard and sugar/honey. Add a good pinch of salt and pepper. Sneak in some fish sauce.

Cook one cup of quinoa on the stove top with any stock - bring to boil, cover, low heat for 15 minutes, rest 10 minutes. Fluff and toss in a big bowl.

Dice half a tomato and half a red onion, into the bowl. Cover a cob of corn with wet kitchen paper, microwave on high for 4 minutes. Slice the kernels off the cob, into the bowl. Chop up a bunch of green herbs of your choice, into the bowl.

Mix with dressing. Taste, adjust.

Top with something hearty: avocado, eggs (hard boiled, onsen, ramen, pan fried all good), haloumi cheese.

And then something crunchy - kale chips. shredded coconut, goji berries, pumpkin seeds, almond flakes, croutons, corn chips, poppadoms, crackers, soy crisps.

Restaurant-Level Japanese Curry.

The thing about 'restaurant-level' curry, is <u>the stock.</u>

Most steak restaurants in Japan offer curry during lunch because they have plenty of bones for stock and off-cuts for meat. Water alone, according to the packet instruction, won't cut it. You should use beef/pork/vegetable stock, make your own or even instant bouillon cubes.

Just remember - <u>any stock is better than water</u>.

The second important thing is <u>the caramelised onions.</u> If you ever feel like your homemade Japanese curry is not 'deep' enough or lacking some 'oomph', <u>caramelise the onions</u>. If you have cookbooks saying it takes 15-20 minutes to caramelise onions THROW THEM AWAY NOW. It takes 30-45 minutes onwards to fully brown the onions on a low to medium heat. (High heat will burn them.) Try adding some balsamic vinegar, sugar and water towards the end.

Another trick I read from a Japanese magazine is to <u>grate the carrots</u>. It increases the surface area and makes the stock sweeter and thicker like a smoothie. You can skip this, but if you're going to caramelise the onions, you have time to grate some carrots.

Another pro tip: <u>mix your roux</u>. My favourite is *Java Hot* and *Golden Curry Hot*. You can also make your own roux from scratch, but that's another recipe in itself. One method I use to trick my Japanese wife is to mix in some Malaysian curry powder/paste. Because the typical Japanese spice tolerant is piss weak,

Caramelise the onions,
grate the carrots,
mix the roux, and go
crazy with umami.

anything extra like cayenne, garam masala, chaat masala, togarashi, S&B curry powder, Chinese five-spice etc will elevate the 'curryness' of this ... curry. It'll make them go 'wow'.

Don't forget to finish with an umami thickener - a tbsp of fish sauce, or Worchester sauce, yakisoba sauce, oyster sauce, tomato paste, all good. Want some curveballs? Grated apple, dark chocolate. Everyone but Australians look away - vegemite.

The basic Japanese curry hero ingredients are potatoes, meat, onions and carrots, but you can add any ingredients you like - tofu, beans, mushroom, broccoli, cauliflower... are all ok. Just add them and cook for another 5-8 minutes before you add the roux.

The roux already contains a fair amount of fat and seasoning, what we're doing is just to boost the texture, colour, complexity and umami.

There's no wrong way to make this.

Yakiyakisoba.

The biggest hurdle of making yakisoba at home is that you'll never ever get the pan / wok to be as hot as the hot plate to emulate the 'char' or 'wok hei. So pro tip: <u>we fry the noodles and the ingredients separately.</u> Essentially frying in two batches. This applies to all homemade stir-fry noodles.

Cook the noodles per packet instructions. At this stage in my life, I do not care if it's a proper yakisoba noodle. I use egg noodles, Shanghai noodles, udon, rice noodles... Cook them and drain according to your liking, drizzle 1 tbsp of sesame oil plus 3 tbsp of the yakisoba sauce*. Mix well, set aside.

Heat up the pan. Roughly chop up the proteins - sliced pork belly / bacon / chicken / firm tofu, into a medium heat pan with vegetable oil. It will take 2-3 minutes for protein to brown, so if you haven't already, now's the time to julienne the vegetables. The default is onion, carrot, capsicum and cabbage, but we know it's whatever that's left in the fridge - green beans, mushrooms, asparagus, broccolini... Once the proteins turn brown, add the vegetables and 2 tbsp of yakisoba sauce per person. Once they're slightly charred at the corners remove from heat and onto a plate. Set aside.

Crank the heat up to high, add 1 tbsp oil and add the noodles in the pan. The key here is to get the noodles crispy. Move the noodles around to prevent soggy bits. Non-stick pans are not recommended.

First yaki - fry
the proteins and
vegetables.

Second yaki -
fry the noodles.

Return the veggies to the pan. If you're using beansprouts, this is the time to add them in. Mix thoroughly.

Taste the dish. Too salty? Add some water. Taste the dish. Not enough flavour? Add more sauce. Taste the dish. Too dry? Add more water. Too wet? Scramble.

Transfer to a big plate, serve.

Add your gourmet toppings.

My wife adds bonito flakes, aonori (overpriced dried seaweed), a disgusting amount of Kewpie mayonnaise and chilli. I like to add a fried egg with fish sauce, lime juice, and some sambal belachan.

*You can buy yakisoba sauce in most Asian groceries,

OR: whisk together 1 part each of teriyaki sauce (soy sauce, mirin, sugar), worcestershire sauce (Japanese says 'wustaa sosu'), oyster sauce, tomato sauce. 100g should be plenty for 2.

Oyakodon =
Scrambled Eggs on Rice.

Say to your spouse: "bae, tonight we're going to have scrambled eggs on rice."

She'll think you have brain damage from all the social distancing.

Say: "hey honey I'm making oyakodon for dinner tonight".

She says: " Oh lala *anata*, let's open that bottle of expired sake we bought from Japan."

Oyakodon is exactly that - <u>scrambled eggs on rice with teriyaki sauce</u>. I know that, you know that, she doesn't have to. So shh.

Let's prep - first, cook rice to your liking - short grain, long grain, basmati, I don't care.

Slice 2 chicken thighs* to bite size chunks, marinate in 1 tbsp each of soy sauce, mirin, sugar and sake. Whisk 3 eggs, set aside. Prep the sauce - whisk 100g dashi (or any stock) and 2 tbsp each of soy sauce, mirin, sugar.

In short, 200g of equal part teriyaki sauce and stock.

Set aside. Now we wait for the rice.

Tenkasu
before tamago.

*It's chicken by default because the name *oyako* plays on the cruel fact that both parent and child are in the dish. No one says you can't use sliced beef, pork belly, tofu, mushrooms or grilled vegetables with this dish. Remember, we are making scrambled eggs here. Serve it on top of toasts, add bacon and haloumi cheese. No one's judging you. The spouse is not real.
You really do have brain damage.

Slice 1 onion and prepare some greens. The Japanese calls for mitsuba or shisho leaves, but coriander, spring onions, parsley, celery leaves, all good.

Brown the chicken on a medium heat pan with oil.
I like my meat with a bit of char on the edge but you can adjust to your liking. Set aside.

Add the onions into pan, saute until soft. Add the stock mixture and let it come to boil. Add the chicken.

Pro tip: scatter a handful of tenkasu - Japanese fried tempura bits. It'll add volume and flavour to the dish.

Scatter half of your egg mixture. Purists will say DO NOT disturb the eggs, some say scramble hard for even heat distribution. I say do whatever you want, it's scrambled eggs on rice.

Once the eggs start setting on the pan, add the remaining eggs, turn off the heat and cover for 2 minutes. Let the residual heat do the work so the eggs are slightly runny on top. Adjust if you like it really runny, or fully cooked through.

Scoop out your eggs and place on a bowl of rice. Garnish with your greens. Add togarashi, chilli, peri-peri sauce.

Eggs, Garlic Chives.

Have you tried Malaysian Char Kuey Teow?

The best part of CKT, for me, is the burnt eggs and the garlic chives. Take these two ingredients away and you lose the essence of the dish.

The Japanese call this niratama, the Chinese call it jiu cai chao dan. Whatever man, you want to claim a dish with two ingredients? It's a race to the bottom.

Chop a handful of garlic chives (roughly 150g) to 2 cm length. Rinse, pat dry.

How my wife likes it: beat 3 eggs and whisk with 2 tsp soy sauce, 1 tsp sake / cooking wine, 1 tsp mirin.

How I like it: beat 3 eggs and whisk with 1 tsp Cheong Chan cooking caramel, 1 tsp fish sauce, 1 tsp Shaoxing wine.

Heat 1 tbsp oil in a wok / pan to high heat and toss the garlic chives in with a pinch of salt. Keep them moving until wilted. Toss the garlic chives into the egg mixture.

<u>Pro tip</u> - the hero of this dish is not garlic chives nor eggs - it is the oil.

Hot oil.
How hot? Smoking point hot.
How much? About 1 tbsp per egg.

The oil should be
so hot that the eggs
fluff up immediately.

We want the eggs to immediately fluff up with giant blisters when you pour them in instead of sticking to the wok/pan*.We want to deep fry the bottom of the eggs so they are crispy and fluffy around the edges yet still runny on top without burning the chives.

Use chopsticks or spatula to scramble it.

If you do this right it should all be over in 60 seconds. If you like really runny eggs, maybe even less as the residual heat will continue cooking as you slide it out on a plate to serve. Cook longer if you like your eggs well done.

This is an easy last-minute side dish.

I personally think it's better than the Japanese tamagoyaki egg rolls.

There, I said it.

* Speaking of woks and pans this is where a carbon steel / cast iron / stainless steel pan comes in. Avoid non-stick pans for high heat. You have been warned.

Longevity Noodles.

Speaking of garlic chives, have you tried making Chinese Longevity Noodles?

The Chinese serve this to celebrate one's birthday. For me, the 'longevity' now refers to my own life. As a parent, this Chinese version of Cacio e Pepe with five ingredients is a lifesaver.

You can easily find 'longevity' noodles in Asian Groceries, but any noodles are fine (If using dried noodles, my favourite is the Taiwanese Guan Miao Mian - 關廟面).

Drop 2 serves (200g) of noodles in boiling water for a minute, then chill in ice bath, drain, drizzle and toss with a tbsp of oil, set aside.

Finely dice 2 cloves of garlic, prep 100g of bean sprouts and chop 50g of garlic chives into 2cm stripes.

Heat up the wok with 2 tbsp oil, add garlic. Once fragrant, add noodles, cook for a minute or two. Paint 2 tbsp of soy sauce around the edge, mix well. Add garlic chives and bean sprouts. Toss until everything is wilted and glossy. Taste, adjust seasoning, top with black pepper.

Plate up. Serve as a side dish, a main dish, a midnight snack. A last-minute picnic addition.

*If you're feeling fancy, cut up some proteins, fried tofu or eggs.

Gyoza Pro Tips.

Gyoza is extremely subjective - everyone has their own opinion about how a dumpling should taste. There are so many recipes online nowadays, I trust you can find one to your liking. What I'm offering here are just the pro tips.

1. Salt, squeeze and drain the cabbage.

Always salt the chopped cabbage in a colander for 15 minutes then squeeze them dry. This prevents them from getting 'watery' and messing up the seasoning. If you're using wombok / Chinese cabbage, get ready to lose 50% of your veggies lol

2. Infuse aromatics with oil.

For the longest time, the garlic and ginger in my dumplings just tasted 'raw' and I always thought my products weren't good enough. The solution? Infuse them in 2 tbsp of oil under low heat for five minutes. This will better incorporate the flavours with the fillings.

3. To Shaoxing, or not to Shaoxing

This is up for debate. I used to skip point 1, so whenever the cabbage liquid mixed with the wine, it just smelled off and I've avoided ever since. I also believe, in the past, people used Shaoxing to mask the 'meaty' smell. Nowadays it's nostalgia, ingrained in our Asian memory, like kansui to noodles.

4. Fat, fat, fat

The secret to juicy dumpling fillings is not juice, but fat. My fillings are usually quite lean (chicken and prawn mince) so I will sneak in a rasher of chopped bacon for added fattiness. Xiumai usually calls for pork fat in the recipe. If you're making tofu dumplings, load up with sesame oil. 'I like how your dumplings are so dry!' said no one ever. Pro-tip for vegans: <u>smashed avocado</u>.

5. MSG is shameful, but also useful

1 tsp worth of chicken powder, or Ajinomoto, or miso, fish sauce, chopped porcini mushroom, tsuyuu, teriyaki sauce, or Maggi seasoning is all the difference you need. You know what, I take it back, it's not shameful; umami is just common sense.

6. Microwave the filling to taste test

Microwave or pan-fry a little of the filling and adjust seasoning if necessary. No more guesswork.

* For Melburnians: to me, the best gyoza skin is the A3 brand - I seem to only find them at TANGS along Russell Street, like a rare pokemon. KFL stock them apparently.
Although a little bit thicker, Tak Onn is readily available everywhere.

7. Slurry (Optional)

The slurry ratio of cornstarch to water is 1:10. So add 1 tbsp of cornstarch to 150g water if you want to make that 'webby' crunchy base you see on Instagram. If you put too much cornstarch you're just adding a hot mess of dough onto your gyoza. Nowadays I skip this because the 'web' takes up too much space as I prefer to stuff as many gyozas as possible on the pan. The store-bought* gyoza skins have enough flour to make the bottom crispy.

8. Pan-fry, steam, deep fry.

Start with medium heat in a (preferably) non-stick pan. Pan-fry the dumplings for 2 minutes, then add enough water (or slurry) to fill up to 1/3 of the dumplings' height. Pro tip: after you add the liquid, <u>manually lift each dumpling up</u> to let the water get under so they won't stick to the pan later. It's gonna be tricky (hot fingers!) but worth it. Cover for 4 minutes or until the water is almost gone. Uncover, drizzle 2 tbsp oil around the edges. When the water fully evaporates the oil will fry the bottom to make them crispy, give or take another 5-6 minutes. (Check every 2 minutes and once you get it, just use the timer next time.)

When ready, invert a plate over the pan, flip quickly, and serve with soy, vinegar, chilli oil, yuzu kosho.

Marriage-Saving Spagbol.

Every time my wife considers leaving my sorry ass, she thinks: "hmm but then who's going to make me spagbol?" And she stays on. Marriage is just like work man, if you're ugly you gotta somehow make yourself indispensable and make them think twice before replacing you.

The most important ingredient in this dish is time.

There is no pro tip here - you need a good 3 hours including prep, 12 if you consider the best sauce / curry is always the refrigerated leftovers.

So, prepare a big pot and a big pan.

Make soffrito in the big pot. Dice 3 rashers(200g ish) of bacon(or pancetta), into the pot under medium heat. While the bacon browns and the fat renders, dice (or pulse in a food processor) one onion, one carrot, one stalk of celery, 3 cloves of garlic. Once the bacon is crusty, dump aromatics into the pot, switch heat to low, stir every 5 minutes.

Heat up the big pan, brown 500g of minced meat (30% pork, 70% beef), 1/4 at a time. Aim for brown crusts forming at the bottom of the pan, like a collapsed burger patty. Each batch should take 5 minutes on medium-high heat. So every time a batch is done, set the meat aside, stir the other soffrito pot.

Time.
Patience.
Love.
Fish sauce.

Once all the mince is done, toss into the soffrito pot.
The mixture should look like a caramelised mess.
It's good, trust me. Deglaze the meat pan with 200ml red/
cooking wine, scrape the fond, pour wine into the pot,
scrape the pot. Reduce wine.

Prepare (A): 100ml chicken stock, 1 can chopped tomato
(whole is fine, you just need to mash it), 1 can passata/
tomato puree, 100ml milk, 1 bay leaf (optional), a tsp of
grated nutmeg (optional).

Pour (A) into the pot and stir, half-cover on low heat. Stir
every 20 minutes until the texture reminds you of oatmeal,
roughly 2 hours.

If your pot is cast iron, yay! Transfer into a fan-forced
140°C oven, uncovered. Stir every 20 minutes until the
texture reminds you of oatmeal.

Just before cooking the pasta of your choice,
add to your pot: 2 tbsp tomato paste, 1 tbsp butter, a good
chunk of grated Parmigiano-Reggiano, and, alright fine, a
small pro tip - 1 tbsp fish sauce, and stir.

Cook and drain pasta on plates, drizzle olive oil
and grate more Parmigiano on pasta, top with a big ladle
of sauce.

Garnish with basil/parsley.

Pizza Sheng Jian Bao.

So you have some leftover Bolognese sauce.
Why not make some bao?

I have two bao dough recipes - both stolen. One from
my mother - sweet and fluffy, which I recommend for
savoury fillings; the other from my wife's home econs
textbook - firm and chewy, best for sweet fillings.

Ingredients	Makes 12-16
Cake Flour	300g
Bread Flour	100g
Salt	0.5 tsp
Sugar	25g
Lard	15g
Water (35°C)	150+50ml
Instant Yeast	8g
Sugar	1tsp

Wife's

Ingredients	Makes 12-16
Cake Flour	500g
Baking Powder	1.5 tsp
Salt	0.5 tsp
Sugar	80g
Canola Oil	45ml
Water (35°C)	200 +50ml
Instant Yeast	8g
Sugar	1tsp

Mum's

First, activate the yeast (modern instant yeast doesn't
require this step anymore). Mix yeast, 1 tsp sugar and a
pinch of flour with 50ml of water. 35°C is ideal. It should
take 15 minutes for them to start bubbling.

Mix all the dry ingredients, then wet. Knead with hand
for 15 minutes or a stand mixer until smooth. Proof in a
warm place for 30-45 minutes.

Chewy bao dough for sweet fillings; fluffy bao dough for savoury fillings.

Once the dough doubles in size, punch the dough and deflate it. Start rolling into a long snake. Divide dough to 16 pieces or roughly 45g each, roll into balls. Cover and rest for another 15 minutes.

Now let's make the pizza filling - add shredded mozarella to your leftover bolognese sauce, 1 part each. In fact, use leftover Japanese curry, stew, mapo tofu, bugolgi.

Roll each dough ball into a disc-like wrapper. Place some filling in the middle of a wrapper then fold into a bao shape. I still suck at this, but YouTube is a good learning place. Fold them in half like dumplings if you cbf.

When you're ready, cook it like gyoza - pan fry 1 minute, add water up to 1/4 of the baos, cover for 4 minutes, lift cover, add 1 tbsp of sesame oil around the edges, wait for 6-7 minutes. Sprinkle sesame seeds and spring onions.

Alternatively, you can steam them.

If this is still too much, here's a pro tip:
use gyoza skins.

Still no? How about ready made frozen gua baos from the supermarket?

No? How about burrito?
Jaffles? Toastie?

15-minute Mac & Cheese(ish).

Ready?

1. Empty half a bag of macaroni (or any short pasta) into a pot and cover it with salted water by 5cm. Fire the stove and bring it to boil, stirring to keep the pasta from sticking. Once boiling, remove from heat, cover pan and set the timer for 8 minutes. By not having to boil the water first, we have ninja-chopped 10 minutes off the total cooking time. Pro tip: <u>toast 50g of breadcrumbs / panko in the oven.</u>

2. Meanwhile, whisk together 100ml of milk, 50g of cream, 2 eggs, 1 tsp mustard, 1 tsp of cornstarch, then prep 100g of good melting cheese (200g if you LOVE cheese, we're talking almost 1:1 ratio of pasta and cheese here). I usually have those shredded 3-in-1 cheese in the fridge, but you know - fancy cheddar, young Swiss, Gruyere, young Provolone, Gouda, Camembert ... You get the idea. Cheese. Soft. Melting. Good.

(OPTIONAL) 3. You should have 5 minutes to spare - fry up some bacon and broccoli, or any protein to your liking. In this photo, I used zucchini and mushrooms. Last week it was chicken and frozen green peas. Apply common sense. Set aside.

Oven toasted
breadcrumbs / panko
= mind-blowing.

4. When the 8 minute is up, drain pasta and return it to the saucepan, heat off. Add 50g butter and stir until melted. Add the milk mixture, the egg might scramble if the pan is still too hot, but we're after a quick meal here so I'm not fussed. Add cheese mixture and stir constantly, until the cheese is completely melted and the mixture is silky and creamy. (Add ingredients from step 3 now if applicable.)

Season to taste with salt, pepper. Sometimes I add curry powder, chipotle hot sauce, fish sauce, MORE grated parmesan, you know, anything to boost umami.

Sprinkle crunchy breadcrumbs on top.

This is a lovechild between *Serious Eats'* recipe and carbonara. Since it's mac & cheese, we don't have to adhere to the 'no cream' carbonara commandment - I'm just after volume and goo. Yet, at the same time, there's something really sad about feeding only mac & cheese to my daughter, so adding some bacon and broccoli makes me feel less like a loser dad.

So not really mac & cheese; not really carbonara either.

I serve dinner in 15 minutes, my daughter is well fed, who's complaining?

Jiu Yim (Salt & Pepper) Prawns.

Why you should cook this: it takes 15 minutes to prep, 15 minutes to cook, but your boss will be impressed. In short - low risk, high return. Prawns just have that 'wow' factor across the world.

1. Seasoning: dry-roast 2 tsp salt, 2 tsp pepper and 1 tsp five spice powder in a pan. Remove, allow to cool, combine with 1 tsp sugar, mix well. Set aside.

2. Prep 500g of prawns with shells on - tiger, king, banana, whichever. Pro tip: <u>devein them using the toothpick technique.</u>

3. Prep aromatics - dice 1/2 onion, (red, brown, shallots - same same) 2 cloves garlic, 1/2 capsicum, some spring onions, and chillies for the big boys.

4. Dust the prawns with flour / cornflour / potato starch / tapioca flour.

5. In a deep-fry pan or wok, bring oil to 180°C. Dip the tail of one prawn to test. Fry 2-3 at a time to keep the oil temperature consistent. (I use a cast iron pan and time 1 minute per side.) Remove the prawns and absorb oil with kitchen paper. Repeat with remaining prawns.

Devein prawns with this 5-second toothpick technique:

6. Bring a frying pan to medium heat, using some oil from the deep-frying, add the aromatics and cook until fragrant, sticky and soft. Pro tip: <u>sprinkle a handful of curry leaves</u>. Toss. When you smell it, do a head-bobble.

7. Now add the prawns, tossing as you sprinkle the five spice mix. Coat everything well. Unethical pro tip: <u>add a knob of butter and grate a generous amount of parmesan cheese</u>.

8. Remove the prawns and serve. Scatter something crispy, like prawn crackers, nacho chips, papadums, Mamee snack noodles...

9. Dip with a mix of mayo, sriracha, fish sauce and lime juice. My favourite part is eating the aromatics with rice.

10. And guess what? I just taught you how to make salt and pepper squid, salt and pepper fish, salt and pepper tofu, salt and pepper fried chicken, salt and pepper chips, salt and pepper vegetables ......

Karaage aka JFC Pro Tips.

There's not much left to say about Japanese Fried Chicken. The internet has covered all the bases. Except, maybe:

1. Poke the chicken pieces with a fork to help absorb the marinade. The point of diminishing return for marinading is 4 hours. 2 hours is ideal. 30 minute is better than 15, 15 is better than none.
2. Dry the chicken with paper towels before dredging in flour to avoid sad, soggy chicken.
3. According to *Serious Eats*, sake / cooking wine / vodka is essential for crispy chicken. So add a tbsp to your marinade.
4. Dredge with plain flour (juicy) first, then katakuriko, the potato flour (crunchy).
5. Season the flour - add some salt, pepper, garlic powder, salt, curry powder, paprika ...
6. Bring the chicken to room temperature before frying. It'll speed up cooking time.
7. To avoid a splattering mess, deep fry in a wok.
8. Double-fry it. First at 160°C, for a minute. Then 190°C for 30 second until almost whiskey colour. The thermometer is your friend. You can triple-fry them if you want, but I lack patience.
9. Strain the bits in the oil between deep frying.
10. If serving with citrus wedges, ask for consent before you squeeze them all over the chicken. It's basic courtesy.

Classic Steamed Fish.

If you have childhood memories of a fishbone getting stuck in your throat, then congratulations, you have passed the Asian Voight-Kampff test.

Steaming is the national treasure of Chinese cooking, and the fish is its poster child. Everything tastes better steamed - potatoes, broccoli, rice, dumplings. That's basically the whole business model of dim sum.

If you're not fluent in Mandarin, at least be fluent in steaming. I'd much rather my daughter bring home a banana who could steam a fish than a fluent Asian who can't cook for shit.

So, go to the fish market, find a fish you like, any fish. The fresher the better. I'd avoid blue fish such as mackerel or sardines, but hey, you might swing that way. We usually alternate between baby snapper and barramundi from Vic Market. I don't believe in shop loyalty - just pick the fish you think looks the best on the day.

Wash and pat dry.

Make three parallel cuts on each side of the fish so it'll cook faster.

Get a big plate - make sure it fits in your wok/steamer covered, I learned that the hard way. Crisscross three stalks of spring onion on the plate, like the three musketeers. The theory is that they will lift the fish up to let the hot steam flow through.

Place fish on top, season with 1 tsp pinch of salt on both sides. Slice a knob of ginger and place them in the fish cavity and on top of the slits.

Once water is boiling in the wok, carefully place your fish within and cover. If you don't have a steaming attachment for the work, just place a small bowl underneath. Try making a steaming rack with chopsticks.

For a medium-sized fish (700-800g) I set the timer to 10 minutes. If it's your first time, I'd overcook it and scale (hehe) back the next time. If you have a thermometer, aim for an internal temperature of 62°C.

As you wait, prepare the sauce - 1 part soy sauce to 2 part stock with a pinch of white pepper. It makes more sense to use chicken powder if you're making a small amount. No one's judging here. Add Shaoxing wine if you like. Here's a thought: fish sauce with fish.

Thinly slice up another stalk of spring onion and gather a handful of coriander. Chopped chilli, pickles. All good.

Once the timer's up, discard the wilted spring onions and ginger, pour away the pool of smelly fish liquid without burning your fingers. Use mittens, use that weird Asian folding tongs, use your child.

Heat up a small pan/wok with 2 tbsp cooking oil. As you wait, place the sliced garnish on top of your fish. Once the oil reaches smoking point, pour it over the fish - AWAY FROM YOU, ARMS EXTENDED.

If it doesn't splatter and go TssSaaaAaAa, the oil wasn't hot enough. Better luck next time.
Don't despair, the fish is still good.

Pour the sauce on top. Some like their fish swimming in sauce, some like to drizzle like olive oil, I'll leave it to you.

Serve with rice.

Now you can call me dad.

Here, the cheek's the best part.

I learned everything about steaming fish from this video. Maybe because I grew up in a country colonised by the English, the way Fuschia transitioned from a British accent to a perfect Beijing '生抽' triggers my culinary button all the time.

 Here's the video. I'm not sure the 'bashing' is necessary. The lady says to flip and whack the dough to 'release' the layer. It sounds like a prank to splash hot oil on yourself. But by all means give it a go.

CYB aka Green Onion Pancake.

This isn't even my recipe. It's from an old lady from Youtube. The old lady from Youtube always wins.

Why this Cong You Bing recipe works so well:

First of all, the high hydration - so hot right now. That's 70g water to 100g flour. Insanely difficult to handle. That's why the old lady said to be patient. I found a way to hack it - use a hand mixer. If you have a Kitchen-aid or stand mixer well, ladida, good for you.

The second most important thing is the 'twisting' of the dough before flattening it. Layers, my friend. Layers.

Another cool thing she did was steaming the spring onion pancake halfway after pan-frying one side. The moisture trapped inside the dough tries to escape when you cover the pan, thus creating a fluffly texture.

And how did she finish it? She deep fries it.

Yes, the MOST important thing (which the lady kinda quickly brushed off) is the amount of oil. Don't be coy - when you think you've used enough oil, add another tablespoon. Don't worry man, this is a vegetarian dish.

Feel free to crack and egg or sprinkle some cheese on top when you pan fry them. Why not finish with chopped chilli and coriander with a dash of fish sauce to finish? Or dip them in equal part of soy sauce and rice vinegar?

Throw a piece of kelp (konbu) in the rice pot.

* Then again, the Japanese Agriculture video says rinse the rice in water once, swish your hands around the rice for 20 times, rinse again. The 'cloudy' water is the essence of the taste. I'm telling you, no one has a clue. Everyone is winging it.

Proper Japanese Rice.

I'm not sure if Japanese rice is worth $8 a kilo.
But I do know once you get used to it, it's hard
to go back.

Wash the rice - my wife has a 'goshi goshi' technique
which I can never master. Since the point is simply to
remove the impurities, I rub the rice gently in between
my palms*. Drain the rice in a colander and leave it for 15
minutes. The rice will absorb the moisture on the surface
and turn white.

If using a rice cooker:
I like my rice firm, so I fill it to 90% of the line I'm
supposed to hit. So If using 2 cups of rice, fill to 1.8 mark
of the line. Press play. Fluff.

If using claypot / dutch oven:
2 cup water to 2 cup rice.
Bring rice and water to boil on medium heat, once
boiling, cover and turn the heat all the way to low. Wait
for 15 minutes. Remove from heat source, leave for
another 5-10 minutes. Fluff.

Pro tip: throw a piece of kombu in the pot / pan.
This generates a faint umami note in your rice.

Ever wonder why Japanese restaurant rice tastes better
than yours? Now you know.

AKA 'I don't even want to think anymore' rice.

*The Malaysian in me always wants to add an extra tsp of Cheong Chan cooking caramel / dark soy with some lap cheung and anchovies to make it a 'claypot chicken rice', but I always lose the majority vote. Please try it on my behalf.

Takikomi Gohan aka Lazy Rice.

I know my Japanese friends are cringing right now because to them, this is like cereal.

Influencers be making this with their fancy donabe pots. Sounds like a good idea, until you have to wash the darn thing at the sink. Nowadays, we have science and technology - enter the rice cooker.

Wash 2 cups (~300g) of short grain rice, rinse, set aside. Marinade equal amount of dashi / stock with 2 tbsp each of soy sauce, mirin, sugar, sake, and a handful of bonito flakes in the rice cooker.

Thinly slice 1 small carrot, 50g worth of burdock root (gobo, find them frozen and pre-sliced at Japanese grocery, you can replace with parsnips or turnips), a good handful of mushrooms (shimeji, button, shiitake, enoki, all good).

Slice 1 (200g) chicken thigh / choice of protein into bite sizes, then toss everything into the rice cooker.

Hit play.

This dish is made usually towards the end of the week, when we simply can't be bothered to cook nor order take out. The leftovers are made into onigiris.

The Search for Uncle's Congee.

This one time, in Singapore, at a hawker stall, I ordered congee and watched the uncle dump a giant scoop of gooey rice into a clay pot of boiling stock and thought: cool, I have to look it up one day.

Little did I know the internet had no information on it. The Chinese internet had no record either. It felt like my mind was playing tricks on me.

Know where I found this recipe in the end? A Japanese magazine on Chinese food. Talk about irony.

Soak 1 cup (180g - 200g) of Jasmine rice in water for 1.5 hours (or overnight), drain and dry for 30 minutes. Boil a pot of water.

Add 2 tbsp of neutral oil to a pan (wok is much better) on high heat until hot. When you stir in the rice, it should make a big 'tsssaaAaAaAaAAAAAA' sound. That's right we're frying the rice uncooked. This will infuse the pan (or wok) flavour into the congee.

When it starts to change colour, add 500ml of hot water into the pan, 2 tbsp of Shaoxing wine, stir, turn heat to low and cover. Set the timer to 20 minute, stir from time to time until you get to a gooey consistency. It should stick to your spatula easily when you lift it up. Something about sugar molecules breaking down, science stuff.

Now you have your gooey base.

You can finish it off right now or freeze some for next time.

Now you'll need 1 - 1.5 L of stock. Chicken is standard, but vegetable, fish, dashi, chicken bullion all good. Heat up your stock to a rolling boil, then dump the goo in, ladle by ladle, stir and let rip for 10 minutes or until you're happy with the consistency. Like watery jook? Less goo. Like it thicker? More goo.

Finish with a pinch of salt.

Now you have the default plain congee - 明火白粥.

From here on you're basically in the hot pot zone - pei dan and pork? Chicken and corn? Fish slices? Beef brisket? What's in your fridge? Shredded chicken, salted egg, carrot, tofu, kimchi, mushrooms... I'll stop here, you know what you like.

For me, the absolute cornerstone of a soul-healing, mind-calming Cantonese jook is thinly sliced ginger, spring onion, sesame oil, white pepper and Chinese doughnuts.

Before you take out your pitchfork and say this is not the proper way, or the best way, or your ancestor's way, chill dude, I know. But those recipes are always either too simple or too vague. I don't trust you to share your real family secret. I don't trust my own mum to share her secret recipe.

But this, although from a magazine - it makes sense for businesses. You have the goo as a base and you can change the stock and ingredients depending on order rather than having 15 different pots of congee boiling away in the kitchen.

So it's probably not the most authentic, but I think it's the most consistent. And it has that trade secret / espionage flair to it no? Like, ooh, this is how a Chinese restaurant in Japan does it. Or how a hawker stall uncle does it in Singapore.

So remember: <u>first, make instant congee paste, then add to boiling stock, season and finish with toppings.</u>

Paella is Spanish Fried Rice.

Once, while shooting for a Spanish restaurant during paella night, I asked the chef if they used Bomba rice or Calasparra. He replied 'just regular medium grain SunRice, mate.' That was when I realised paella to Spaniards is perhaps just like fried rice to the Chinese - everything's made up and the rules don't matter. In fact, the original Paella from Valencia did not contain seafood, but rabbit. Not a fan of mussels and capsicum? Take it out.

Finely chop 1 onion, 2-3 cloves garlic and 1 peeled tomato (or 3 tbsp tomato paste).

Prepare 7-800g worth of protein and / or seafood. Chicken, fish, chorizo, prawn, mussels, clams, pippies, blue swimmer crabs, calamari ... your choice. I'm a prawn and chicken guy, so I usually go 200g diced chicken thigh and 200g (8) prawns with shell on, with 100g (a handful) of scallops.

Grind a generous pinch of saffron with some salt in a mortar. Alternatively, soak saffron in 50ml of hot water.

If you replace saffron with turmeric, no judgement here. Just don't touch the darn thing, it will stain everywhere. Pro tip to get rid of turmeric stain: <u>sunlight</u>.

Sunlight is the enemy
of turmeric stains.

Heat 3 tbsp olive oil in a large paella (or frying) pan over medium heat. Fry the onions, garlic, tomato until soften. Add the non-shellfish protein (chicken, fish, squid ..) and 300g short grain rice and stir, making sure everything is well combined.

Add 800ml stock (seafood or vegetable works best), 3 tsp smoked paprika and the saffron salt, stir for the last time.

When the stock boils and the grains begin to swell, lay the prawns and crab on top.

DO NOT STIR THE PAELLA.

Cook over medium heat for about 10 minutes until the stock has reduced enough that you can see the rice underneath, then add mussels and pippies (if using) into the rice and cook until their shells open.

Scatter with some green beans or peas (Spaniards look away: try adding Kimchi!) cook for another 5 minutes over low heat.

Serve from stovetop to table.

Fight over the crispy socarrat at the bottom of the pan.

Pair with white wine.

Mapo Tofu.

Cube 400g of tofu to 2cm. Firm tofu is more flavourful; soft tofu has a better mouthfeel. The proper way is to blanch the tofu to remove the 'soy taste'. I do it for special occasions, say when Halley's comet is visiting.

Tradition dictates the mince to be beef for higher fat content, but I use chicken most of the time. 200g - give or take, I like to make it 1 part mince 2 part tofu.

Prep 2-3 tbsp doubajiang. The 'authentic' doubanjiang is Pixian doubanjiang - super pungent, you have to go to an Asian grocery for that. Chop it down with your knife or a blender because it's pretty chunky. I don't see any problem with *Lee Kum Kee*. Experiment with other brands. You can add chilli to your miso if you want. Use Korean gochujang if you want. Buy ready-made packs. No judgement here.

Aromatics are your standard minced garlic and ginger, 1 tbsp each or adjust to your liking. Slice spring onions to garnish in the end.

200ml stock - any is better than water.

Slurry - 3 tbsp corn starch / potato starch to equal amount of water.

Umami booster - I use 1 tsp of oyster sauce, 1 tsp of fish sauce, 1 tsp of black soy, 1 tsp of zhenjiang vinegar 1 tsp of chicken powder (MSG), 1 tsp of sugar,

Use PiXian Doubanjiang for authentic, pungent mapo tofu.

Adding the slurry in 3 parts gives you control over the thickness of your mapo sauce.

Make the chilli oil* - 2 tbsp of oil in wok / pan under low heat and add 1 tbsp of chopped dry chilli and 1-2 tbsp of red huajiao and 1 tsp of five spice powder. Set aside.

Heat up the wok (low heat again) with 2 tbsp of oil, add the doubanjiang. Once the red oil 'leaks' out, up the heat and brown the mince. Once it starts crisping around the edges, add the aromatics and tofu, stir gently. Add the stock, let it simmer for 5 minutes, add umami booster. Everything should be bubbling.

Taste, adjust.

Pro tip: add the slurry in 3 parts - stir everytime and control the thickness to your liking.

Add chilli oil.

Taste, adjust seasoning.
Garnish with spring onion.

Serve on rice.

* You can buy pre-made chilli oil like *Lee Kum Kee* or *Lao Gan Ma*. (Although, Si Chuan citizens might revolt if you serve mapo tofu without huajiao.) They have powdered form of everything nowadays too - huajiao powder, dried chilli powder, korean chilli powder. All I can say is experiment. Our main flavour will be coming from the doubanjiang, so this chilli oil is really just an extra kick.

Magic Asian Sauce.

The Japanese say 'an', Chinese calls this method of cooking 'liu', most people know this as the 'slimy gooey gravy on top of my Asian dishes'.

It's not radioactive or artificial - just seasoned stock + slurry. It's super versatile, it's magic.

Let's take crispy noodle for example - heat up 2 cups (~500ml) stock, dissolve 1 tbsp each of soy sauce, Shaoxing wine, sugar, zhenjiang vinegar, adjusted to taste*.

In a separate bowl, mix slurry - 3 tbsp corn starch with 3 tbsp water. Set aside.

Look for 'chow mein' noodles in Asian grocery stores. In Melbourne, you can't miss *Tak On* or *Gold Star*.

In a big pan/wok, heat up enough oil to cover the base, once smoking, toss the noodles in and flatten with a spatula, give or take 1-2 minutes. The goal is to make them crispy. Flip, repeat. Tip into your big serving plate.

Now fry up some proteins - chicken strips, beef strips, tofu, prawns, calamari, fishcakes ... set aside.

Next fry some sliced onions, carrots, mushrooms, snow peas, capsicums, gai lan, choy sum, beansprouts etc. until softened. Once the edge is getting crispy, pour in your protein and stock mixture. Stir or give it a few good swirls.

You master the
Asian magic sauce,
you master two pages
of a Chinese
restaurant menu.

Once boiling, pour in your slurry in 3 parts while stirring, creating a mini-tornado.

Seek your desired thickness and once the gravy is bubbling, pour on top of the crispy noodles. Garnish with spring onions or coriander. Add XO sauce / chilli oil / fried shallots / fried onion …

You can also serve the magic sauce on top of rice, or omit the carbs completely and serve as part of a banquet.

Fancy some wa dan ho? Do an eggdrop - scramble an egg and drizzle into the sauce before the slurry, serve with thick flat noodles.

Like black pepper beef? Fire up some sliced beef and add heaps of pepper and oyster sauce.

Why not deep fry some fish and add some creamed corn? Asparagus? Bean sprouts?

Congratulations, you just mastered two full pages of a Chinese restaurant menu.

*The Japanese version - 2 cups (400ml) dashi, 1 tbsp each of soy sauce, mirin, sake, sugar, but you know my good friends - fish sauce, bonito flakes, chicken powder, they will all take good care of you.

XO Sauce.

Look at this sauce.
It looks terrible, yea?
What a hot mess.
You laugh.

But once I bring it to your pot luck, it's game over.
Everyone will be surrounding it - wait, what's this?
What's IN this? What's the recipe OMG I can't stop. Your
mother-in-law is now my mother-in-law.

This is XO sauce, the sauce to hit all gastro G-spots.

How to make one jar:

Soak 50g of dried scallops and 30g of dried shrimp in a
bowl of Shaoxing wine overnight. The wine should cover
all the ingredients.

Drain the scallops and shrimps the next day, reserving
the liquid. With a blender/processor, pulse half an onion
(or 3 shallots), 5 garlic cloves, chillies of your choice,
a knob of ginger and 25g (1 rasher) of *Jin Hua* ham*/
smoked bacon/ prosciutto until fine. We want finely
diced, but not a watery mess.

Next, blend/process the scallop + shrimp to shreds.
You should be able to see strands of scallops, like thick
saffron threads.

The sauce to hit all culinary G-spots.

Pour 250ml peanut (or any neutral) oil in a medium heat pan, add the onion mixture and fry for roughly 3 minutes until you can smell them. Then add in the scallop mixture, stir for 5 minutes.

Add reserved soaking liquid from the shrimp and scallops. Stir gently until bubbling then reduce heat to low and simmer, stirring occasionally, for 15 minutes.

Add 1 tsp each of soy sauce, oyster sauce, fish sauce, 1 tbsp sugar, and cook until desired colour and consistency.

Some like it soggy, like the ones you buy from LKK. I like mine crispy to the point of charcoal, so I finish it off in a fan-forced oven at 120°C for another 15 minutes to avoid overcooking.

This is the WD40 of seasoning.

Your sauce journey ends here**.

* Jin Hua ham is another expensive ingredient that's hard to find and verify its authenticity in Australia. Smoked bacon and prosciutto work just as fine for me. Lap Cheong should work too.

** Unless, you can't take seafood, then my deepest condolences.

Make
this purely
with the sense
of hearing.

I'm not usually an 'organic' guy, but there is a noticeable difference in flavour when compared to the supermarket ones. We're talking about $1-2 difference/kg here. That's way, way less than what movie theatres are charging you.

Popping Corn.

Heat a heavy duty pot on medium heat with a lid,
drop 2 kernels of corn, pour in 2 tbsp of oil.

Once the kernels have 'popped' (usually 3-4 minutes),
take the pot off the heat and pour in enough corn to fill
the base. Shake to evenly distribute the fat and corn,
back on the heat, lid on.

Now we wait. We wait for the pot to build up enough
pressure for the magic to happen.

When the popping starts it's a thunderstorm of happiness
- my daughter's favourite part. The room smells like
childhood and Saturday night. My mouth salivates for hot
cocoa. Your eyes, nose, ears are all activated. Sure, you
can make this with a microwave, but you're shaking the
pot with your biceps, there's heat in the kitchen. Gee, I
wonder what will impress your date more? That's right,
you're welcome.

Once the popping slows down to once every
3-4 seconds, shake the pot one last time and pour them
into a bowl immediately. Don't leave them because the
steam will leave an unpleasant taste.

Melt some butter on it. Sprinkle with some salt, ground
cinnamon, shredded coconut, sugar or honey. Pro tip -
grate some parmesan cheese over it. Grate truffles on it.

Recipe for Melbourne Tap Water:
11.5g   Sodium Bicarbonate (NAHCO$_3$) aka Baking Soda
23.7g   Magnesium Sulphate aka Epsom Salt
964.8g   Deionised / Distilled water

Three Tips for Filter Coffee.

1. <u>It's not you, it's the grinder</u>.
Sorry, there's no roundabout way to say this, but if you spent less than $300 on your grinder, then your filter coffee will never be able to compete with the ones served by your barista. Instead of a leather apron, invest in a great grinder. A great grinder produces a more consistent grind. A great grinder makes $6 beans taste like $20 beans. Are you tired of me saying 'great grinder' yet?

2. <u>Temperature</u>.
Think of water temperature as a volume dial - go full boil if you like floral, acidic coffee; if you want to mute the flavours, add some cold water to your kettle. The rule of thumb is darker roast, lower temperature; lighter roast, higher temperature. Water temperature also affects flow speed. So if you're aiming for that
3 min 30 sec extraction, go full boil. Don't worry, you can't 'burn' the beans. The beans already went through a 200°C roaster, your water is 99°C at most off the kettle. They'll be alright.

3. <u>Water.</u>
At the peak of my coffee-making madness, I was adding baking soda and epsom salt into distilled water to make my own 'Melbourne Tap Water' in Japan*. Think about it, a cup of filter coffee is <u>99% water</u>.
Why are we all neglecting the water? Try mineral water. Try filter water.

* Sugar - you can adjust the
ratio to your liking. I usually
decrease the sugar in the filling
and focus on the crumble.

Caster is fine, brown sugar
better, those fancy rapadura
sugar in cafes? *chef kisses*

Butter is the secret to a crunchy
crumble. If the crumble gets too
lumpy, freeze it for 10 minutes,
adjust with flour, start again.

** You can absolutely take
the crumble further - add
teaspoons of ground cinnamon,
ground ginger, oats, coconut
flakes, almond flakes...

If you're making savoury muffins
- replace sugar with grated
cheddar cheese, parmesan
cheese, diced bacon, pepper,
thyme, chives, garlic powder,
onion powder, sesame seeds ...

Muffin Top.

I know you know the best part of the muffin is the top crust. We don't really care about the filling.

The pro tip for muffins is the crumble.

2 parts flour, 1 part sugar, 1 part butter*.

Depending on the batch size, I usually start with 60g flour, 30g butter, 30g sugar.

Similar to making pie crust, cube the (cold) butter, toss and mix with the flour and sugar with your hand. Pinch and rub with your fingers until they become pebble-like. If you can go finer to a breadcrumb texture, even better. It'll take 5 minutes on top of your usual routine. Even your child can do it.

Scoop some on top of your muffins just before placing them into the oven.

Congratulations, you have unlocked the ability to bake OMG-I-just-ate-five muffins.

Apply this to any recipes you find on the internet.

Remember, it's all about the crumble**.

Beat the egg whites separately to make fluffy Japanese hottokeki.

(One) Pan Cake.

Pancakes are mythical food, implanted by pop culture and false advertising. I can count with one hand the number of times throughout my life someone actually made me pancakes for breakfast, and that's including my mum.

The usual pancake recipe is pretty straightforward - whisk 2 eggs, 250ml milk, 250g self-raising flour, 85g caster sugar, 1 tsp baking powder. The not-so-straightfoward part is to wait 1 hour for the batter to rise. Who has time for that?

So pro tip: <u>pour all the batter* into a well-oiled cast iron pan, and chuck it into the oven.</u> Let's put the 'cake' into pancake.

180°C, 20 minutes.

The crusts are golden, top and bottom crispy, fluffy in the middle. Slice it up like pizza. Top with maple syrup, berries, jam, bacon.

Pro tip: <u>beat the egg whites separately to medium peak with handmixer before folding into batter.</u> Watch them fluff up. They charge you 2000 yen for this pancake in Japan.

* Also works with any pancake mix. The Japanese hotcake mix from the Asian grocery? *chef kiss*

The Secret Behind
Shredded Cabbage.

I once saw a guy shave a whole ball of cabbage using a
sashimi knife in a yoshoku restaurant in Kobe. For the
longest time, I thought to make shredded cabbage
I need the Japanese knife, the Japanese skill.

Until I found out about the Super Benriner Mandolin.

Ever wonder how fine dining restaurants serve you
consistently thin discs of radish/carrot/cucumber?
They use the Super Benriner Mandolin. I shouldn't be
surprised. My mum had it since the 80s. I just assumed
restaurants have, you know, superpowers.

So I shredded a ball of cabbage with the mandolin. It's
thin, but the texture is not right. They weren't crunchy.

*It MUST be the Japanese cabbage! It's terrior, like how
the best red wine must be from France. Australian
cabbages suck!*

And then I found a tip on the internet - soaking the
shredded cabbages in a big bowl of ice bath for 15
minutes will crisp them up.

So I ice-bathed my shredded cabbage. Fine, they're
crunchy now, but they lack sweetness.

*It MUST be the Japanese cabbage! It's terrior, like how
the best red wine must be from France. Australian
cabbages suck!*

Mandolin,
ice bath,
sugar.

I gave up.

A few years later I brought it up with a friend who used to work in restaurants in Japan. He just said:

Sometimes, Japanese cabbage, not good.
For sweet cabbage, we add sugar.

ARE. YOU. FUCKING. KIDDING. ME?

The purpose of me swearing isn't to say how restaurants are deceiving us, but to show how much authority we give to a third party, to the ingredients, and how little faith we have in ourselves when it comes to cooking.

The only good advice I saw from Marco Pierre White was from an old Youtube video of him yelling 'taste! taste! taste!' to a young Gordon Ramsay.

Even behind closed doors, chefs trusted their own tongues; not recipes.

How simple is that?
You want thinly sliced cabbage? Use a mandolin.
You want them crispy? Ice bath.
You want them sweeter? Add sugar.

Bonus

After I sent the book to print, I continued writing
and posting to *Subtle Asian Cooking*.

Here are the additional essays and recipes that did not
make the cut for the first print run. Either because
I don't make them as often as the other dishes,
or they broke my own rule of no long-winded backstories
and unwanted fat / trimmings.

You have been warned.

Ants Climbing up the Tree.

There are no ants; it's fried vermicelli.
Why don't they just call it vermicelli? Ah, then we won't
be having this conversation, will we?

The story probably went like this: some poor farmer
takes care of his sick and yet loving mother because you
know, RESPECT YOUR ELDERS. Although he had little to
no ingredients, he made up a creative name, so she ate
them all and he's a good son and everyone lived happily
ever after.

OR, an emperor stumbled across this dish while in
disguise as a peasant and he loved it. His eunuchs didn't
have the heart to tell him it's meat and vermicelli so they
made up a name on the spot. The emperor stole it and
made it a permanent dish in the palace. I think.

You know what? We don't care.
It tastes great, the name sticks.
It has gone viral in our collective minds - into the history
books.

Seriously though, this is my personal favourite Sichuan
dish. It's so basic, so peasant, so much easier than
pasta. There I said it.

This is also a great practice for mapo tofu because the
flavour profile is essentially the same. You master this,
you master mapo tofu.

So prep 100g of minced protein - beef is the default for
its fattiness, but go pork, go chicken, chickpea, beans,
tofu, tempeh.

Have 200ml stock or water with bouillon/stock cube on standby.

Finely dice half a carrot and half a capsicum. Mushrooms, fried tofu, fishcakes, feel free to join us it's a leftover party!

Finely dice 2 cloves garlic + your preferred amount of ginger.

2 tbsp of Pixian doubanjiang. You can use other brands like Lee Kum Kee but Pixian is the real deal. They are pungent and super chunky. Pro tip: use a blender, or finely dice them on the chopping board with your knife. I used only 1 tbsp for my lunch yesterday because I didn't want to blind my daughter with chilli oil fumes, so adjust the doubanjiang to your liking.

100g (2 bunches) of Long Kou* (龙口) vermicelli. Package instruction says to soak in water for 15 minutes. I usually blanch them in hot water then soak in iced water.

Now heat up the wok, 2 tbsp oil.

Low heat is the key here.
If you've tried making mapo tofu and witnessed your doubanjiang burnt into black sticky bits, you know what I'm talking about.

Add your chopped doubanjiang, stir around.

Now is a good time to open the windows.

Once you see red oil seeping out when you scoop them up with your spatula you can add the garlic and ginger. Stir for a minute.

Add the mince, diced carrot and capsicum, 1 tsp of sugar and turn up the heat to medium-high, stir again until cooked through.

Pour in the stock.
It should fill all the way up, covering the mixture.
Stir again.

Now add the vermicelli. STOP the stirring.
The temperature of our home cook wok /pan has dropped immensely from the added stock and vermicelli - if you stir now you'll get a sticky mess.
We don't want that. Let the vermicelli slowly soak up the liquid and temperature.

Instead of stirring, add seasoning - 2 tsp each of shaoxing wine, and soy should do. Add a tsp of zhenjiang vinegar if you feel inclined. If you can't get the Cantonese out of you, a tsp of oyster sauce. Some can't live without a tsp of black soy, that's ok too.

When the mixture starts bubbling, then we stir. Stir and make a small tornado in the wok. Release your inner iron chef. Toss it. Combine well.

Taste, adjust seasoning, add a tbsp of sesame oil.

Stir again for a minute or two.

The stock should have reduced by now. The vermicelli glistening and see-through. If you like it wetter, add water, or more sesame oil.

Stir, taste, adjust seasoning.

Plate up, top with spring onions.

That should be enough metaphorical ants for two.

* Long Kou vermicelli is usually made from mung beans, some have broad beans in it. I'm not entirely sure if they have proper QC like your Reggiano Parmesan or Champagne from Champagne. But if you're standing in an Asian grocery store aisle feeling lost and confused, go with the one that has 'Long Kou' printed on it.

So right until we add the vermicelli, the procedure is the same as making mapo tofu (alright fine, there's no carrots or capsicum or what not, and mapo tofu has black bean sauce and thickener), but this is a great introduction to Sichuan cuisine.
Once you master this, then you can graduate to mapo tofu.

It has three combo punches of spice, flavour, texture.

If you ever thought of mastering a vermicelli dish, start with this one.

Honeypot Cacio e Pepe.

What's the deal with pasta, right?

The time it takes to boil the water and another 10 minutes to cook it makes you regret not going after a packet of Shin Ramyun. It's an anglicised Indomie. A really long-winded chong you ban mian.

So, then, why do we make pasta?

Because pasta is what separates men from the boys.

Think about it. You've just Netflixed and chilled, and the lady says she's hungry. If you say 'let's Indomie', that means you're cheap. What are we? Fresh off the boat in Uni? If you say 'lets Uber Eats something', that means you only know how to solve problems by swiping on the phone. Typical new-age men.

But you say "Let me make you a Cacio e Pepe".

Wait a minute. Pasta? Italian? Now that's a curveball.

Cacio e Pepe (cheese and pepper) is made from pasta, cheese, salt, and pepper.

Rock out the small pot you usually use for making instant noodles, fill it with water, bring to boil, salt it good, like a proper tablespoon.

Wait a minute, aren't we suppose to cook pasta in giant 4L pot? Nah, that's what shops that sell giant 4L pot want you to think.

Smaller pot = water boils faster. Besides, we need the thick starchy pasta water for later.

Take 200g (2 generous serves) of spaghetti, break them in half. Italians nonnas be screaming, but by breaking the pasta in half they will fit in the pot, preventing you from pushing and twisting them in.

Now set the timer to 1 minute less than the package instructions. Stir the spaghetti. Smaller pots mean they stick easy, so stir them well.

In another pan, pour in 2 tbsp of olive oil/butter, medium heat, scatter in 1-2 tsp of coarsely ground black pepper, you should be able to smell it in less than a minute. Remove from heat, set aside. Pro tip: <u>Add Hua Jiao, try Sichimi.</u> Why not curry powder? Garam masala? Gochugaru powder? Not only are you resourceful now, but you are also cultured and well-travelled.

Stir the spaghetti again.

Grate 50g of pecorino cheese. You can go half Pecorino Romano and half Parmigiano Reggiano. One's sharper made with sheep's milk, the other nuttier with cow's milk. Set aside.

With 1 minute to go on the timer, scoop in 50ml or 3 tbsp worth of pasta water into the pepper pan, add another tbsp (15g) of butter. Mix well.

When the timer goes off, check if the pasta is to your liking, use tongs and transfer into the pepper pan. Don't worry about making a mess, it's good. It shows how carefree you are.
Toss the pasta. Add the grated cheese, in 3 parts. The heat from the pasta should be enough to melt the cheese. Stir and toss until you reach a creamy consistency. If the cheese clump together, add more pasta water and stir.

Taste, adjust seasoning. Toss again.

Make sure the creamy sauce coats each strand of spaghetti. You want the sauce to almost drip but still clings on towards the end.

Plate immediately. Drizzle some fine EVOO.
Sploosh.

Carbs from durum wheat, creamy fat and umami from the cheese, a nice little kick from the pepper.

Get it? Pasta is the difference between a one night stand, and a committing relationship.

Nowadays all you need is a credit card to attain a Rolex or whatever. But a fridge with Pecorino Romano? Parmesan Reggiano? De Cecco no.12? Maldon Salt flakes? Cultured butter? You can't fake that.

Not only are you skilled, but you also appreciate the simple things in life. You also have the balls to offer a dish made from 4 ingredients. It shows you care enough to cook her a meal from scratch, to be vulnerable.

If you fail, then you will look like the biggest idiot in the world. And maybe that's alright. At the beginning of any relationship, the girl just wants to see you stumble, even if you're the heir of a Korean zaibatsu. She wants to know that you will struggle and risk looking like an idiot ... for her.

IF you succeed, then you're father material. She can trust you to take care of the children in the future, maybe share the chores - through thick and thin, sickness and health.

If this is not the ultimate subtle Asian flex during early dating, then I don't know what to say. Maybe she's lactose intolerant.

So practise, practise, practise.

I've taught you marriage-holding Bolognese, now this is the honeypot Cacio e Pepe.

But the most important advice here, man, is learn to love yourself before you attempt to love others.

Relationships come and go, your favourite instant noodles or restaurant might go under, but the skill to make Cacio e Pepe will stay with you forever.

Why Your Okonomiyaki Suck.

Because you don't have <u>yamaimo</u>. It's Japanese mountain yam (sometimes called namaimo) that makes the Japanese pancake toro toro - thick and sticky.
We don't have it fresh in Australia.

If you're in Melbourne, Fujimart in Prahran sells a frozen paste version. Sometimes, you can find yamaimo powder (Otafuku brand) at Japanese grocery stores. Call them, if enough of us ask for it, they'll find a way to bring it here. OR look for the pre-mixed Okonomiyaki flour. Read the labels - the good ones will have mountain yam in it.See note below*.

Whisk 80g flour, 160g of yamaimo, 2 tsp of soy sauce, 60ml dashi / any stock (or 1 tsp dashi powder with powder mixed with 50ml water) until sticky, chill in the fridge for 30 minutes.

While you wait, shred or finely dice 200g (roughly a quarter) worth of cabbage, sprinkle with salt, place in a colander. After 15 minutes, drain, squeeze the moisture out.

When the 30 minutes is up, whisk 2 eggs, mix together with the cabbage and chilled batter.

Do you know why your okonimiyaki suck?

<u>Because you didn't use tenkasu and sakura-ebi.</u> Pour in 1/2 bag (60g) of the fried tempura bits into the mixture, save the other half for oyakodon or udon noodle soup. Sakura-ebi is the tiny crispy shrimps - scatter a generous handful.

Now you have enough batter to cook two generous servings of Kansai-style Okonomiyaki that doesn't suck so much.

The default protein is sliced pork belly. Australian butchers don't do that. You can try the Asian frozen pork belly made for hot-pot, or freeze and slice your own. But why not try bacon, pancetta, salami?

Like making a pancake, heat up a big pan (with enough space to flip) medium heat with oil. Ladle half the mixture, spread evenly with your ladle/spatula. Place enough pork belly to cover the top, push them into the wet batter with your finger, wait 2 minutes, flip. Wait another 2 minutes, flip again. Check if your protein is crispy enough, cover and steam for another 2 minutes.

The bigger and thicker your batter is, the longer you need between flips and steaming. Adjust accordingly.

Now, the sauce - if you're using store bought sauce, no judgement here. Just in case you can't find any, mix 2 tbsp ketchup, 2 tbsp Worcestershire sauce, 1 tbsp oyster sauce and 1 tbsp sugar.

Plate your Okonomiyaki, ladle the sauce on top of the protein side, squeeze some kewpie mayo, create some mayo art. One time in Osaka, this guy drew a Doraemon (I think) on my Okonomiyaki.

If you fail, don't worry, we're going to cover it with a big handful of katsuobushi (bonito flakes) and a good pinch of aonori (dried seaweed), the umami cornerstone of Okonomiyaki. If you really want, you can add red pickled-ginger. I'm not a fan, because it's mostly colouring. We're not eating sushi here, so I'm not sure why restaurants even serve that.

Now dig in quick. This dish makes you sad when eaten cold.

*This code covers most of what you need.

For a name that translates to 'grill whatever, man', the Japanese sure expect this dish to be done in a specific way. Don't believe me? Then tell me why do they all look and taste the same in restaurants?

As long as you have the sauce, kewpie mayo, and bonito flakes, you're pleasing 90% of the Japanese tastebuds. In fact, I'm not even sure the batter matters. Undercook it, burn it, they can't see it anyway - just smother it with sauce.

Seriously, once you make the batter, go crazy. Add prawns, add squids. Vegetarians should try mushrooms, beansprouts, garlic chives. Skip the cabbage altogether, add kimchi and you get buchimgae. No sauce or mayo? Try soy, vinegar, fish sauce, chilli, top with coriander, spring onions.

This recipe even uses cup noodles, which represents the true spirit of the dish.

Remember: whatever, man.

Dal.

So imagine walking into an Indian grocery in Melbourne. You approach the old lady behind the counter and ask for 'dal', to which she replies:

'Vhich one - Toor, Urad, Mung, Chana? '

A penny drops and you realise you have asked for the equivalent of 'noodles' in an Asian grocery. 'Pasta' to an Italian nonna.

You want to say 'c'mon auntie, dal in a Malaysian mamak store lah' but you know you are a racist because you think all Indian dishes are the same therefore all Indians are the same.

You walk out in shame, or rather, you compensate by buying all the dals on the shelf, then walk out in shame.

You go online and learn about different dals from different regions of India. You learn about tempering, about grinding the spices with your dusty hipster coffee mill.

You go back and buy more ingredients - ghee in a no label plastic container. Black mustard seeds. Samosas from the bain-marie. The lady recognises you now because you're the only chubby Asian asking about basic stuff her son doesn't even care about.

She gives your daughter free poppadoms.

She complains about her husband to you.

10 years later, you still don't know her name, or which dal you're supposed to use in the first place.

In a pressure cooker heat up 600ml water (stock is better). As you wait for it to boil, dice (or blitz) 1 onion, 1 tomato, in the pot. Add 1/2 tsp each of turmeric powder and chilli powder.

Rinse 200g of Toor or Chana Dal, add to the pot, stir, close the lid, pressure cook for 5 minutes, quick release. If the soup seems thick, add water; too thin, let it simmer more. Season to taste. Note: if you're not pressure cooking, soak them overnight and simmer in the pot for 30-40 minutes. Adjust cooking time depending on dal size.

In a separate pan, heat up 3 tbsp of ghee or butter. Add 1 tsp each of cumin seed and mustard seed. Add 3-4 cloves of grated/crushed garlic and 1-2 slits of green and/or dry red chilli. The smell should transcend you to somewhere far away by now, but focus, eyes on the pan. Keep the heat relatively low and stir, if you burn the garlic, start again.

Now add 1/2 tsp garam masala/curry powder, another 1/2 tsp chilli powder if you want, and now a pro tip so your Indian friends be making the Obama face: a pinch of asafoetida (hing). The thing smells like crystalised armpit BO but trust me. Stir one last time, heat off, pour your tempering mixture into the dal pot, taste it, season, stir again.

Now, optional pro tip, do this only if you're marrying into an Indian family: burn a piece of natural charcoal on your stove until it turns red, in a heatproof bowl/aluminium container/ metal box, lower into the pot, pour a tsp of oil / ghee onto the hot coal, see it sizzle and smoke, cover for 1-2 minutes. Remove. Chinese have wok hei; Indians have hot coal in a box. Your Indian family will still shake their head, but they will appreciate the effort.

Taste, season, stir again.

Serve as a soup on your bread, rice, croissant, spring onion pancake, Chinese doughnut. Add a dollop of sambal if Malaysian, but then it'll make you crave a good crispy, flakey roti and a proper amber teh tarik too.

And then you'll cry because you'll always be chasing a shadow. Like that time in university when you did not just kiss the girl while she had her head on your shoulder, you idiot.

Honeypot Pasta II.

Back when my wife was not my wife and we weren't living together, she was busy starting her company and did crazy hours. I'd text her, 'There's leftover pasta' and since my place is closer to her work, rather than taking the train home to Shin ramen, she'd come over, have her dinner and I'd train back with her.

(Sometimes she stayed over, fufufu~)

That's right, this is honeypot pasta - the sequel.

You know the movie Chef, which Happy made Black Widow that spaghetti after work? This is EXACTLY that.

I make this pasta so often, almost once a week.
It's one of the first dishes I learned that didn't suck.
It's intimate and personal because it's. so. boring.
I'd never serve this to my guests.

I learned to make this one dish over and over again and eventually found someone to share it with over and over again. I hope you have such a dish or such a person in your life too.

Bring a pot of water to boil.

Finely dice/grate 4 cloves of garlic,

Cut a packet (250g) of cherry tomatoes in half, squeeze out the juice and seeds, reserving the juice. Combine the tomato pieces with the juice, garlic, 100ml of olive oil, 1 tbsp of red wine / white wine / balsamic vinegar, a pinch of chilli flakes, a few slices of anchovies.

Whisk, combine, emulsify. This is your sauce base.
You can heat it up and toss with cooked pasta as is.

BUT.

We need protein: 4 rashers of bacon sliced, diced, or baton, up to you. Notice we did not salt the sauce, because bacon = salty. If you're using other proteins - chicken, prawn, tofu or mushrooms, remember to salt them accordingly.

We need greens: the original recipe from *River Cafe* calls for 400g zucchini cut into matchsticks, placed in a colander, scattered with the sea salt, left for 15 minutes, then squeezed and pat dry. By the time you're done the pot of water should be boiling rapidly.

Salt the water, drop 400g of De Cecco no.12 spaghetti. Set timer to 10 minutes.

Brown the bacon / proteins on medium heat.
They should be ready after 5 minutes.

Vegetable option B: if you did not bother with the
zucchinis, you can chop up some broccoli/broccolini/
cauliflower and toss them in the pot together with the
pasta with 3 minutes left to go.

Once the protein is done, pour in your sauce. The pan
should sizzle. Swirl, mix. Turn heat to low.

When the 10 minutes are up, check doneness, then
transfer pasta (and veggies if using option B) into the pan
with tongs.

If you also DIDN'T bother with the broccoli, here's your
last chance: quickly grab a big handful of spinach and
toss it in together with the hot pasta.

Mix well. Add pasta water if needed.

Divide into 4.
Grate parmesan.
Drizzle more olive oil if needed.
Tear basil leaves.
Forks out.
Mic drop.
You rock.

Soft Power Jap Chae.

Charge $30 for pasta, no one bats an eyelid; charge over $10 for Chinese noodles everyone loses their shit. Why?

Soft power, that's why.

'Soft power' is a political phrase coined in the 90s to explain a country's power of shaping the preferences of others through appeal and attraction, rather than coercion or force.

In short, it is marketing, seduction, cultural influence. It is propaganda in the form of 'not propaganda'.

Look at Korea.
Since the 90s, the Korean government has invested BILLIONS into its entertainment industry.

If you think all our mums watching Dae Jang Geum was pure coincidence, think again.

If you think Korea and Japan won the 2002 World Cup Soccer host by fair assessment, think again.
If you think Gangnam style went 'viral' by chance, think again.If you think all Asian girls have the same hairstyle as Black Pink because of 'organic growth', think again. If you think Parasite won the best picture last year because it was the best foreign movie … ok that's probably fair, but JSA, Memories of Murder, Sympathy for Lady Vengeance, Mother, Old Boy, Burning, The Handmaiden and many more movies would like you think, think again.

Soft power, man.
It is also why Korean groceries are so dang expensive
in Melbourne.

Don't get me started with the roasted sesame oil.
Do you know why I know Beksul is the best? Because they
don't sell the big cans in Melbourne. They force us to pay
$7 for a 110ml (3 oz) bottle. (What is this, sesame oil for
ants?) The Ottogi 1L tins are like $35 a litre. I've seen
cheaper ink cartridges for printers.

Why?
Soft power, that's why.

I'm angry, yet also secretly proud as an Asian to go, fuck
yeah, Italian have their EVOO in that corner, we have
Korean sesame oil in this corner. The Japanese Kadoya
brand comes close, but it's kinda different.
I won't use it for Korean cooking.

But honestly, I buy Korean sesame oil simply because no
one else does roasted sesame oil better.
It's amazing, it smells like peanut butter.

Trust me, skim on the rest, but not the roasted
sesame oil.

It is the secret to japchae - nay, it's the secret to
Korean home cooking.

Once I was hoping to score some tips from the chef while shooting for a Korean restaurant. He simply pointed towards his giant bottle of Beksul, which till this day I cannot find.

Japchae, for me, is the Korean aglio e olio.

4 ingredients - dangmyeon noodles, roasted sesame oil, sugar, soy sauce. They're the founding flavours to the easiest introduction dish to Korean cooking.

The rest is just personal preference. There's no wrong way to make this because the name translates to 'freestyle veggies'. It's chop suey, it's rojak, it's japchai. It's salad, but palatable for Asians.

So, 200g dangmyeon in boiling water for 4-5 minutes, shock in ice bath, drain, set aside in a bowl. Marinade with 2 tbsp sesame oil, 2 tbsp sugar/honey, 4 tbsp soy sauce. Set aside. I add a tsp of rice vinegar. Also optional: garlic.

Cut the noodles up with a pair of scissors.
Apparently, we are ok with cutting Korean noodles, but it's blasphemy when we cut pasta.

Why?
Italy has stronger soft power, that's why.

Let's make this a vegetarian dish today shall we?

Finely slice A - onions, carrots, black fungus/mushrooms, spinach and tofu.

Prep B - bean sprouts, garlic chives.

Heat oil on the pan, stir-fry A until crispy on the edges. Set aside.

Pour noodles and marinade into the pan, mix well. It should be glossy and shiny.

Add B into the pan. Mix well for a minute or so, until the garlic chives and bean sprouts are wilted but not soggy.

Add A again, stir.

Taste, adjust seasoning.
Plate up.
Salt bae with sesame seeds.

See your vegetarian friends lose their shit over this vegetarian Korean potato noodle stir-fry.

Why?

Soft power, that's why.

Lost Bread - Pain Perdu

Ok, fine, it's French toast.

Remember how I said homemade pancake is a 'myth' dish - often heard but seldom seen in real life? Easy to visualise, but hard to execute? French toast is the complete opposite.

Stale bread? Yes, I always have two slices left. (Although, allegedly the best French toast is made with Jewish challah bread, fluffy white Japanese milk bread, or brioche. Fat and sugar, mmm.)

Whisk 2 eggs, 100 ml milk, 1 tbsp sugar, 1/2 tsp each of vanilla essence, a little ground cinnamon, grated nutmeg, tiny bit of salt.

Soak the bread slices in the mix for 5 minutes. If your bread is relatively fresh, you might need to dry them out overnight, or chuck them in the oven at 100°C for 10 minutes or so to prevent the bread collapsing in its own weight. Think getting out of a pool with your wet clothes on, oof.

Heat enough butter to swirl around the pan, fry each side for 1-2 minutes under low-medium heat, until you see your desired colour.

Serve with fruits, bacon, more eggs. Top with maple syrup, honey, icing sugar, yoghurt, ice cream.

MIL-Approved Tomatoes, Eggs.

Dads generally like a good show. A big steamed fish, a crackling pork belly, a full slab of char siu, sous vide Wagyu, a giant roast chicken, bottle of wine with an old fashioned cork that goes 'zoonk'. He's the 'big ideas' guy. He looks at you and his biggest concern will always be 'is this joker capable of taking care of my daughter?'

Mums are generally immune to those things. She's seen all the tricks in the book when your dad was busy courting her. Her dad probably wondered the same thing about her husband. At the end of the day, she's the yin to your father-in-law's yang.

Your mother-in-law doesn't care if you're capable; she wants to know if you're reliable.

How do you prove that?
You make tomatoes and egg stir fry - 番茄 / 西红柿炒蛋.

You snicker, you cringe, you snort.

It's ok.I'll wait here while you scour through all your cooking heroes/gatekeepers/authorities/sugar daddies on the internet - The New York Times, Gourmet Traveller, Adam Liaw, Serious Eats, Epicurious, Fuchsia, Good Food, Marion, Hetty, Wang Gang, Omnivour's Wok of Food52... search for 'tomatoes, egg'.

Did you find it?
See what I mean?

All of them, every single one of them, has a tomato and egg stir-fry recipe. And they usually go like this:

1.   Quarter your tomatoes, set aside.
2.   Whisk an equal number of eggs as tomatoes, season with a pinch of salt and vinegar.
3.   Heat up the wok with oil, scramble eggs until slightly firm, remove immediately.
4.   Oil the wok again, add the tomatoes on high heat, season with sugar, stock and a little bit of ketchup, wait until the tomatoes break down into mush, within a minute or two.
5.   Add corn/potato starch slurry until thicken, add eggs, mix well, taste, season, plate up.

Why is this dish so omnipresent? Why is everyone sucking up to this simple dish?

Firstly, it's a no brainer - the simple marriage between natural MSG from the tomatoes, and fat + protein from the eggs. Sweet, sour, salty, fulfilling.

The other reason is its historical relevance - when wars were fought, and revolutions were rampant, when money was being made, when the country was being built, destroyed, occupied, rebuilt, behind closed doors, literally, the back of house, ALL Chinese mothers, their mothers' mothers, were making tomatoes and egg stir fry for their children.

No one's going to say it, but this is the true national dish of China. The representation of its humble beginnings. This dish reminds us of a time when the Chinese invented gunpowder, paper, printing, the compass, soccer.
It's in our blind spot because it's too easy.
Too obvious.

We like to make things complicated, to have 8 major cuisines from different regions and 108 dishes from the Man Han Banquet which the emperor took 3 days to finish.

For every convoluted Chinese fusion dish ham-fisted with truffles, wagyu, foie gras and caviar, we long for something simple like the tomato and egg stir-fry.

The yin to the yang.

Man, how I wish I could be there to witness the first Chinese to taste an egg dish combined with this weird red persimmon brought in by the foreigners. (番人+茄子=番茄, get it?)

If you want to show your understanding and eagerness to maintain your Chinese/Asian root to your mother-in-law, you will make and serve her this dish with a bowl of rice.

She will raise her eyebrows.
Balsy, she'll give you that.
She's probably made this dish twice as often as the amount of rice in her bowl.

She tastes a spoonful.
She pauses. Something's different.
Something's missing.
She takes another bite.
She's processing.

Eventually, she lets out a gasp.
It startles your father-in-law.

"You removed the tomato skins!"
"As usual, mum, nothing gets past you," you say.

During your mise en place, you've scored the bottom of the tomatoes in a cross pattern and submerged them in boiling water for 10-20 seconds, before transferring to an ice bath and peeling the skins off.

Without the skins, the dish has a better mouthfeel, a subtle elegance to it. The human body can't digest them anyway.

You've elevated the most simple dish there is.

But not because of ego.
You did it for your wife, your daughter.
Also for grandma, because it's easier to chew.

And THAT, is how you show you're a reliable

son-in-law.
Not by showing off and buying shiny things.
But by respecting the history, the culture, by cherishing what you currently have and improving the little things in life.
You don't replace what (who) you love, you improve it constantly, you grow with it.

Now, don't you dare think this ends with you taking a bow in the spotlight.

The only right way to end this is to say: " But mum,
I'm still not happy with my seasoning. Maybe next time, you can show me how to cook your version. I want to replicate this dish for your daughter,
and maybe your granddaughter can learn together with her po po too."

Face, bro, you gotta learn how to save it.

There's more than one way to drop the mic.

Roll credits.

Yoyo Ma plays the cello.

Most Difficult Cake In The World.

The single most frustrating object for a home cook to bake is the Japanese Cotton Cheesecake.

Macarons? Croissants? Croquembouche? Sure, those are difficult, but we *expect* them to be difficult. You go to culinary school, you wear aprons and chef hats to make them in fancy ovens.

But the Japanese Cotton Cheesecake? This JCC?

Behind its unassuming appearance, hides a competitive underground sport.

Not for the Japanese, no, they walk into an Uncle Tetsu or Uncle Rikuro and pay money for it.

It's for the Asian aunties like your mum.

For them, this is the UFC of home baking. Their quest is to make the most perfect, fluffiest, non-collapsing Japanese cotton cheesecake, and post it on their blogs (yes, blogs) to show off their affluence.

Don't trust me? Google it.

In fact, the most searched and proven recipe belongs to Craft Passion (2017), which was modified by I shoot I eat I post (2014), which was inspired by Diana's Dessert (2004).

They always start by saying it's easy.
Super easy.

That's how they get to you, like a reverse-psychology MLM pyramid scheme.

She even made it in your kitchen. Your mother, using basic ingredients - cream cheese, egg, flour, sugar, all home brand. From Aldi.

Your daughter loves it.
Nai Nai's fuwa fuwa cake, she said.

Then one day, you decided to make it yourself.
How hard can it be, right?

You fail spectacularly.

But because you're Asian and you're too proud to ask your mum, you troubleshoot that shit.

You fail, again. This time it cracked.
The cake is laughing at you.

Still, the fault can't be on you. You, the highly educated sophisticated food photographer. You, the only normal cousin within the family tree, started measuring your oven temperature. It must be the recipe. But just to be safe you buy some rubbish gadget to separate the yolks from the white. You make sure you beat the eggwhites right. You even measure their weight.

That darn thing finally rises.

"I got you now motherfucker," you said, only to find it collapsing when you turn off the oven.

And on your 7th failed attempt you start to question reality. This is not some Heston Blumenthal El Bulli dish; it's something made by an Asian auntie, your mother, IN YOUR KITCHEN. With caged eggs for god's sake.

After failing your 12th attempt, you 'casually' gave her a call.

After talking about the weather and some formality you finally sneak in a question: "so do you sift the flour when you make that whatchamacallit cheesecake you made here last year?"

You can't see it, but you know she's having that look on her face. That same look Buddha gave when Monkey King said he urinated on five giant mountains somewhere so far no one would ever, ever know - I got YOU now motherfucker.

Slowly, over time, she feeds you random advice.

First, you need the right 20cm cake tin. The ones that don't come off with an attachment. It has to be completely sealed. Do you have the right tin? No? Then wrap aluminium foil under it and pray it doesn't leak. Also, don't butter the tin. Use baking paper to surround it.

You failed attempt no. 15.
You tried lowering the temperature this time - it just became a flat and dense looking pound cake. You've seen better dog faeces.

Did you make sure the cream cheese, butter and milk come to room temperature? You need to make sure you have a water bath in your oven. You need to make sure your meringue is somewhere between soft and hard peak. Too soft; it won't rise; too hard, it'll collapse.

Attempt no.19 - unsuccessful.

You need to make sure you fold, not stir, FOLD all mixture lightly. If you go too hard, the cake will collapse; if you don't fold enough, it won't rise consistently and you'll have the big cracks.

You failed attempt no. 21.

Never use the convection setting - top and low heat only. Also, place the cake at the lowest rack. Did you do the low-temperature then high-temperature method (110°C for 20 min then 160°C for 25min)? Or the high-temperature then low-temperature method (180°C for 20 min then 140°C for 25min)? Or the 150°C, then 130°C, then 110°C method? Did you check the cooling period? Some say you should leave the oven door ajar by sticking your glove / a chopstick in the last 30 min. Some say just leave the cake in the oven until room temperature. Did you bang the tin right after taking out of the oven? It will prevent it from collapsing. Did you take it out from the water bath? The hot water might overcook the bottom.

Attempt no. 24, you lost patience and didn't fold it quite right this time. You knew it's not gonna work before you put it in the oven.

Did you use cream of tartar to stabilise the egg whites?
Did you give the mixture one last stir with a toothpick?
Did you make sure the baking paper isn't too high to block
the oven? Did you? Did you? Did you?
Is this her way of trolling, or simply asserting control
over your adult life? Is this how she gets you to talk to
her? Is she enjoying this? You don't know what to think.
Eventually, you stopped talking to mum.

It is now your 30th attempt in 3 years. You now know the
sale cycle of the twin-pack Philadelphia cream cheese at
your local supermarket.

Your wife said 'it's ok they still taste good'. She might
as well slap and spit on your face. Cream cheese, sugar,
butter taste good from the fridge. The whole point of
baking is alchemy. You just want it to puff and fluff, and
stay there without cracking. IS THAT TOO MUCH TO ASK?

Emotionally, you're in a foetal position.

You still bake, but not for love. Not anymore, you do it out of
habit. Muscle memory. As you whisk you wonder how did it
end up like this? Was it to prove that you're better than your
mum? Better than the strangers on the internet? Is it self-
expression? Is it an inferiority complex - just to prove that
you can? How far will you shift the blame? A new mixer? A
new oven? You don't even finish the whole cake anymore,
you give it away to friends.

Attempt 42. Still collapsing over the top.

You finally accepted that you have no one to blame but yourself. You're weak and useless and will never amount to anything in life. If you can't bake a basic cheesecake at home, what right do you have to chase your dreams, raise a daughter, find happiness?

So after some counselling and meditation, your therapist says serenity comes when you trade expectations for acceptance.

Maybe, like what your wife said, no one really cares as long as they have a cake that tastes ... 'ok'.

This is probably why basque burnt cheesecake just became the new salted caramel. Because someone decided to go 'fuck it' and let the whole thing burn to bits.

You have come to accept that golden, fluffy, non-cracking, non-collapsing cheesecake exists in your mind. On the internet. On your long list of ASMR YouTube videos of perfect JCC with Korean and Japanese subtitles. Maybe even on your Facebook group.
Just, not in your immediate reality.

And then, suddenly, one day, there it is.
The perfect Japanese Cotton Cheesecake.

Fluffy, jiggly. Non-collapsing.
Shimmering in the afternoon sun.

Yet, weirdly, you don't feel a thing anymore. That little part of your brain and heart that controls excitement, has died a long time ago.

Lost in time, with tears of butter.

You don't even know what you did right, or wrong for that matter. You make some apricot jam, take a photo.

And move on.

You are now a philosopher.

You thank serendipity. This cake is simply a mirror, a reflection of a fleeting moment.

The cake is life - the process is easy, but also fragile, complicated. Teaching you to understand yourself, and simply to cherish the opportunity to have the emotional and financial capacity to bake.

To be present.

It has always been the journey. The intention.

Maybe, one day, when your mum is no longer with you, you'll make it when you think of her. Maybe, you'll keep making this cake for your daughter, and one day when she becomes a surgeon or a judge, you'll sneak in a conversation during Christmas and when her children love it so much, you will feign surprise.

Maybe, you will say:

"Oh, your mum has never made this for you?"
"But it is SO EASY!"

Tea Talk.

Alright, final recipe:

5g Chrysanthemum flower, 5g Burdock Root, 5g Goji Berry. 500ml boiling hot water. Steep for 5 minutes.

Perfect tea after a meal and some afterthoughts:

<u>Taste! Taste! Taste!</u> Only you know what you like. All recipes are merely a guidance, a starting point.

Trim the ends of garlic cloves, and quickly press / whack them with the side of your knife until you hear a 'crack'. The skin will fall off easily as you peel.

<u>Baking soda is amazing.</u> Add 1 tsp with 100ml water and soak with your protein for 15 minutes. It tenderises beef and firms up prawns. Add a tsp into your boiling water and potatoes will crisp up when you put them in the oven. Bake a tray of baking soda in a 140°C oven for 60 minutes and you get *kansui* powder to make ramen noodles. It also makes a great cleaning agent with vinegar. If you burnt your pot (not aluminium), bring water to boil and add a tbsp of baking soda for an hour.

<u>Instagram food is NOT real food</u>. Consider how we shoot food professionally: we figure out the lighting. Then we prep the food. Then we decide on the props. Then we take a photo. We decide we need more props. We switch to the nicer bowl. We brush some cooking oil to make everything appear glossy. Then we switch angle. We take a photo again. After 45 minutes, we get one good shot. Now ask yourself: would you eat the food we just shot?

Ever wonder why tomatoes in restaurants are crunchy, flavourful and yours are always a watery mess?
<u>Salt your cut tomatoes in a colander for 15 minutes</u>, then drain the juice.

Ever wonder why diced cucumbers in restaurants are crunchy and yours are a watery mess? They <u>core the watery seeds</u> out. You can too.

Try grating a little bit of <u>apple</u> with your onions. It will add a sweet tangy complexity to your dishes.

<u>Start cooking mushrooms with enough hot water to cover them in the pan</u>. When the water is almost gone (~5 minutes), then add fat, aromatics, seasoning.

Compared to an industrial kitchen, our woks at home are like bunsen burners. Don't expect to serve a plate of fried noodles in 60 seconds like in the YouTube videos. Double that, triple that.

<u>Taste, taste, taste.</u>

'Organic' doesn't mean it's better, or healthier. It doesn't even mean the farmers or workers are being treated ethically (that's 'fairtrade'). The only concrete fact we know about organic produce is that <u>they are more expensive</u>. Not saying don't buy organic, but taste, compare, then decide if it's worth it.

Add <u>konbu</u> in rice, in soup, in noodles, in water, in marinades. Blend with salt. It is nature's MSG.

<u>Brine / season all your proteins</u>. Salt bae your chicken / steak / tofu immediately as you arrive home and let it dry in the refridgerator overnight. It'll make life better. Trust me.

Want to remove the powdery sulphur layer from the surface of your berries and grapes? <u>Massage with a tbsp of flour and some water, then rinse</u>.

<u>Read the labels</u>. Sometimes the recipe is all on the jar / can / bottle (ratio, sugar content, fat content, etc.) and the only difference is the additives and preservatives.

Vegetable trims - the offcuts from onions, celery, carrots, herbs stalks... <u>save them</u>. Chuck them into your pasta water. It's like mini vegetable stock.

<u>The perfect recipe does not exist.</u> Our pans are different, our burners are different, our humidity, measuring spoon, produce are different. Don't be discouraged just because you 'failed' a dish on the first try. Just like dating, give it three chances before you decide if the recipe is for life.

Fear not the woman who practised 10,000 dishes once; fear the woman who practised 1 dish 10,000 times.

<u>Taste, taste, taste.</u>

Likes Can't Cure COVID-19.

But they do provide an excellent dopamine hit. When Melbourne was struck by a stage-4 lockdown, as shallow as this sounds, I admit the overwhelming support from the SAC group gave me emotional comfort, a distraction. I still don't know why my posts are well received. Some came for the recipes, some came for the writing. It didn't matter. It was my escape, my therapy. I suspect most members are the same - seeking comfort, support and healing through home cooking, and shitposting.

I'm happy when people like my recipes, happier when they actually made the dishes, happiest when they say the tips work.

So I thank my family who gave me the reason to cook. Then COVID-19, who gave me a reason to materialize the recipes. Then my friends and all the strangers from the internet for the encouragement. Thank you all.

Cook more, stay well, and for the love of Buddha, <u>stop paying for Teriyaki sauce.</u>

Sorry for all the grammatical
and punctuation errors.

Instead of a proofreader,
I spent all the money on
tote bags.

Hana-chan, if you're reading
this from the future:

daisuki xxoo.